AIDS ACTION

AIDS Action

Dr Patrick Dixon

ACET INTERNATIONAL ALLIANCE
and
OPERATION MOBILISATION

Three previous editions, entitled *AIDS and You*
This edition published 2010 by
ACET International Alliance
P.O. Box 588, Brentford, Middlesex TW7 9BA, UK;
and Operation Mobilisation.

ISBN: 978 0 9547549 3 8

Editions in English, Thai, Portuguese, Czech, Romanian,
Hungarian, Spanish, Russian, Turkish, Estonian, Paite, German, French,
Polish, Nepalese, Hausa, Igbo, Yoruba, Swahili, Luganda, Amharic, Hindi
– with other translations being made.

To Sheila,
my best friend, closest advisor
and source of endless encouragement for over 38 years,
and to all who have been part of the ACET family
for the last 22 years.

CONTENTS

ACCESS AND LANGUAGE

Please note we have tried to make this book easy to read for people for whom English is not their first language. Most of the book is written in a basic form of English, using around 2,000 different words. We have tried to use only short words and to avoid abbreviations. So, for example, 'antiretrovirals' has been shortened in many places to 'antivirals', while things like MTCT (Mother to Child Transmission) have been lengthened to a suitable phrase. Some words like 'HIV infected' can be stigmatising in certain situations and we have tried to be sensitive with the words we have used.

WHO THIS BOOK IS FOR

AIDS Action aims to challenge churches and Christian individuals to respond in practical, caring and more effective ways. It aims to encourage a global people movement to change our world.

Over 350,000 copies of earlier editions of this book (AIDS and You) have already been given to key workers in 21 languages. All over the world, people have used this book to help start new work or strengthen existing HIV projects. My prayer is that you will find it useful too.

AIDS Action has a special focus on the poorest nations. It shows ways in which different churches and faith-based organisations are responding in these parts of the world, as they are often hardest hit by HIV. They are places where most pastors and priests base their teachings on the Bible, respecting the traditional teachings of the church.

AIDS Action includes lessons from many different projects over more than two decades, and pointers as to what *you* can do.

Maybe you have a completely different outlook on life, a different kind of faith or no faith at all. I hope you too will find this book a helpful and inspiring guide as to how churches and Christian agencies are working in partnership with secular organisations, governments and other faith-based groups to save lives and to help support those affected by HIV.

I am very grateful to George Verwer and Ray & Joy Thomas, who insisted this resource be developed. George Verwer has been our greatest supporter and encourager in getting these books to those who need them most. Thanks also to Paul Kabunga, Marek Slansky, Peter Fabian, Ray Sangqu, Yvonne Kavuo, Dr Sujai Suneetha, Richard Phillips, Sheila Dixon, Calle Almedal, Rachel Ashley-Pain and Hazel Vinson for many comments, suggestions and contributions, and to Isabel Carter for help with editing. Thanks to many others who have contributed their stories or experience as acknowledged on various pages. Finally thanks to Sally Smith at UNAIDS for suggesting this latest edition and for her vision to see the resource available in many more language editions and throughout the world.

All responsibility for errors or omissions is mine. If you notice any please email me: patrick.dixon@acet-international.org

- Please help us by completing the Feedback Form at the back of this book. Your views will improve the next edition, and help our sponsors understand the value of their support.

FOREWORD
by Michel Sidibé – Executive Director of UNAIDS and Under Secretary-General of the United Nations

This book is a valuable resource for faith based organizations and other AIDS service organizations in uniting against AIDS. The book challenges church leaders of all denominations with a strong and urgent call to compassionate action, to eliminate stigma and discrimination and contains practical steps that can be taken by faith-based communities to break the growth of the AIDS epidemic. It is written primarily by and for evangelical Christians, and as such the perspective and presentation at times differs from those of UNAIDS. But we are united by the common purpose of stopping AIDS and in the belief that humans are created equal and enjoy equal rights.

Today, it is possible to prevent mothers from dying and babies from becoming infected with HIV. We can reduce all new HIV infections to zero. We can provide treatment to all those who need it. We can remove punitive laws, policies, practices, stigma and discrimination that block the AIDS response. We can empower young people to protect themselves from HIV. We can stop violence against women and girls. We can prevent people living with HIV from dying of tuberculosis. We can prevent drug users from becoming infected with HIV. We can prevent men who have sex with men from becoming infected with HIV. We can enhance social protection for people affected by HIV.

One important focus of all our work is to eliminate the prejudice, stigma, and discrimination that still prevail in too many societies against people living with HIV and people who often end up pushed out to the margins of mainstream society such as migrants, ethnic minorities, men who have sex with men, drug users and sex workers.

Another is to take concrete action against the injustices and inequalities that fuel the spread of HIV. It is unacceptable that society continues to tolerate the suppression of women and girls, and to do so

11

little to protect them from violence and associated risks of HIV infection – in the street and at home.

Faith, in all its forms, can help transform the AIDS epidemic. We are entering a new decade of the global AIDS response with the spirit of 'We can'.

AIDS: URGENT ACTION NEEDED

AIDS is a major health issue that demands an urgent response.

- One in every hundred people in our world aged 15–49 years is infected with HIV, the virus carrying AIDS.
- More than 33 million people are living with HIV today.
- Every year 2.7 million more are infected, mainly in the poorest parts of the world.
- In parts of central and southern Africa around 1 in 5 young adults are already infected.
- More than 15 million children have been orphaned and an additional 2 million are living with HIV.
- Each year 430,000 more children become infected.

With your help, the future can be different.

A shocking story

All those who start HIV projects have their own personal stories. Here is mine. I will never forget the first person I met with AIDS: a young student in London in 1987. I was visiting the AIDS ward for the first time, where I had been asked to give advice on helping relieve symptoms in those who were very ill.

> More than 80 million people have been infected by HIV already – if you include all those who have already died.

He was desperately sick in a hospital side room – anxious, sweaty, fighting for every breath, and full of fear. He had an oxygen mask over his face and tubes running into his body. He was totally alone in a depressing room and about to die. I was shocked that anyone should be left by themselves, in such a state, in a London teaching hospital. But that's how things were back in 1987, before new treatments and better training changed the lives of so many others with HIV.

His family didn't even know he was ill (he was afraid they would reject him) and the medicines he was getting were doing little to relieve his suffering. It was as if 30 years of hospice experience had been thrown out of the window.

I was trained as a cancer doctor, looking after those close to death at home. For several years I kept my distance from AIDS – it was not an illness I was naturally drawn to; in fact the opposite. But when I saw for myself the reality, the shocking rejection of sick people by doctors, nurses and other care workers, I realised I had to get involved. Skills that some of us had in the care of those dying of cancer needed to be used urgently to help those in the advanced stages of AIDS as well.

> One in six new infections is in a child – many are babies infected during birth. Most of these infections can be prevented.

Here was a human being made in God's image, in great need. How could I respond other than to care and help, laying aside any personal feelings I might have had about lifestyles and the means by which the virus had infected cells within his own body?

That young man died peacefully on the same hospital ward, several days later, with the right treatment and with his loving family by his side, but the whole episode shook me deeply. I would never be the same again.

We started in our home

Back then, not one of 100 cancer hospices in Britain would accept someone with AIDS. HIV was labelled then (incorrectly) as a virus which was passed only between men who had sex with men. Some nurses refused to visit the homes of people with AIDS. Some of the doctors in my country also refused to prescribe the right medicines, because they said they did not want to waste their government budget on people with HIV.

But it wasn't just care workers who were rejecting people with HIV. The church was also caught up with finger-pointing and moral debates, and was taking very little practical action. I had been just as bad in some ways, finding every excuse not to get involved with this strange new illness. And then I realised how heartless I had been, and how my attitude had to change radically.

HIV is different. Not just in how it spreads, or the way it hides for years before people become seriously ill. No other illness provokes such hostility, anger and fear, as well as feelings of shame and guilt. I don't know any other illness where people get attacked or even killed in some parts of the world because others think they might carry the virus.

That young man's death led directly to a support group starting in our own home. We trained members of local churches to help those with HIV who wished to stay out of hospital. We also started visiting schools to teach young people about safe living. Soon a team of nurses, social workers and volunteers was providing 24-hour home support across London, and the work in schools spread across the nation. Today you will find ACET programmes in 23 nations, each managed by local people, meeting local needs in different ways and helping prevent the spread of HIV – just a tiny part of a huge global response by churches and Christian organisations to HIV.

This book was first published in 1989, to encourage practical, compassionate responses to HIV by churches of every denomination, particularly in nations which have been affected most. It was a short version of my first book: *The Truth about AIDS*.

The truth about HIV

What upsets me is that many lessons from the late 1980s have *still* not been learned. Many still think that it will never happen to them. Prejudice, stigma and fear also remain in many places – inside the church as well as in the wider community. Hundreds of millions of people around the world still know very little about AIDS and how HIV spreads.

> Many African nations have been very seriously affected, with huge numbers of grandparents looking after children whose parents have died.

The epidemic is still new compared to most infectious diseases. Doctors still have a lot to learn. HIV is hard to track because AIDS takes years to develop after infection. A vaccine or a cure is still many years away.

HIV surprises many people in the way the virus spreads. For

example six out of ten new HIV infections in African nations are in women. In many nations a woman's greatest risk is being in a long-term sexual relationship, even if she is completely faithful, because so many men are infected from previous relationships, or are unfaithful. A woman is significantly more likely to get HIV from an infected male partner than the other way round. The good news is that people with HIV can now live healthy lives for many years, if tested early enough, and if they get the best treatment. In wealthy nations, people with HIV can live longer than people with many serious chronic illnesses if they take antiviral drugs. However, these medicines must be taken for life under regular medical supervision, as they can have dangerous side effects.

Around 10 million people needed antivirals in 2008, but only 3 million were getting them. In poorer nations these antivirals are still too costly, despite huge price cuts. Most people with HIV will only get treatment from government programmes that provide free antivirals.

Christians have led the way in developing effective HIV programmes in many nations

Christians have been at the forefront of community responses to HIV for over 20 years in many nations. Archbishop Desmond Tutu estimates that churches and Christian organisations provide over 60 per cent of care within HIV community programmes in South Africa. In India the Christian response to HIV has mobilised well over 25,000 workers, part time or full time, in prevention and care. This is a remarkable achievement, a people movement across the nation. We know this through the Christian AIDS National Alliance (CANA) in Delhi, a network of several hundred Christian agencies.

We also see it in hundreds of faith-inspired development organisations like Tearfund, World Vision, Operation Mobilisation, Samaritan's Purse, Dorcas, Christian Aid, World Relief, the Salvation Army, Catholic Relief Services and CAFOD.

Christians from every tradition in every nation have united easily in two simple aims:

- Unconditional, compassionate care for all affected by HIV.
- Effective prevention, respecting and upholding the historic teachings of the church.

World Situation in December 2008

Global estimates	UNAIDS

No of people living with HIV in 2008
| |
--- | ---
Total: | 33.4 million
Adults: | 31.3 million
Women: | 15.7 million
Children under 15 years: | 2.1 million

People newly infected with HIV in 2008
| |
--- | ---
Total: | 2.7 million
Adults: | 2.3 million
Children under 15 years: | 430,000

AIDS deaths in 2008
| |
--- | ---
Total: | 2.0 million
Adults: | 1.7 million
Children under 15 years: | 280,000

So often in the past, as Christians reacting to HIV, we did nothing except to rush to open our Bibles or look to the teachings of the church, to declare that something was wrong. Yet in our responses we often lost sight of God's mercy, love and forgiveness, and the reality that many had been infected through the actions of others rather than their own behaviour. It was possible to be technically correct in interpreting God's standards yet terribly wrong in our own attitudes.

> HIV has already infected 1.5 million people in the US, with 56,000 new infections every year.

Take the example of Jesus with the woman caught in adultery. It is really the story of the missing man. Here is a group of angry men, looking for an excuse to murder a woman, yet two people sinned and the man is nowhere to be seen. Jesus cut right through them with just one sentence: 'If any one of you is without sin let him be the first to throw a stone' (John 8:1–11).

No one moved. Jesus stared them all out until they all left one by one, the oldest first. In one sentence Jesus totally destroyed any possibility of judging others according to a ranking of sin. All of us have sinned and fallen short of God's glory; all are utterly dead outside of God's grace (Romans 3:23).

When it comes to pointing the finger, Jesus forbids us to put ourselves on a pedestal. He was the only person on this earth who had the right to condemn, yet he says to the woman, 'Neither do I condemn you.' He also adds, 'Go now and leave your life of sin.'

As Christians we get confused between the two things Jesus said: either we rush to make moral statements, tripping up over judgemental attitudes along the way, or we rush to express God's mercy and love, falling into a deep hole where there is no longer a clear moral framework. The Jesus way is to hold infinite love and perfect standards in tension together – something we need his help to do.

We know that the traditional teaching of the church, based on Scripture from Genesis to Revelation, is that sexual union is a wonderful gift, as a celebration of love and friendship between a man and woman committed together for life. God designed us as sexual beings.

So how do we live with these tensions? The way of Jesus is clear: we are called to express the unconditional love of God to all in need, regardless of how they come to be so.

Suffering because of HIV

Involved in an HIV project in Hyderabad recently, I was moved to tears as I saw many tribal people from very poor and marginalised backgrounds with HIV. They come in each day and find peace, love and acceptance. Someone touches them, maybe for the first time since they were diagnosed. It is common for people with HIV in many places to be rejected by their families, friends, fellow workers, wider communities and even doctors and nurses.

> UNAIDS estimates that 1 million people in Russia are living with HIV – 60 per cent of them under 30.

The clinic started almost by accident as a leprosy doctor and his wife found people with AIDS knocking on the door of their home. Often they were sent by local church leaders and escorted by members of the congregation. Soon up to 60 new people were coming each month and the family needed desperately to find a place for a clinic. Three years later they had helped over 3,000 people, with a small, dedicated team of staff and volunteers.

Some patients travel up to 200 miles to the only place they know of where they can get treatment without charge. The clinic team also helps people get care from local hospitals. It takes diplomacy, tact, patience and sometimes strong words to help people fight for their rights.

In many nations, people with HIV are regularly refused care, stigmatised, beaten or worse. HIV is often connected with things like poverty, ignorance, low status of women, rape used by soldiers as a weapon of war and lack of access to basic healthcare. That's why we need a broad 'holistic' approach to HIV as part of a complex situation.

Tackling HIV is key to tackling other health problems. The UN Secretary General Ban Ki-moon said in 2008 that how we tackle HIV 'will impact all our efforts to cut poverty and improve nutrition, reduce child mortality, improve maternal health and curb the spread of malaria and tuberculosis'.

Leaders in denial – in church and wider society

Even in countries where the level of HIV is overwhelming, people often slip into denial. I was shocked recently to talk with senior team members of a university in South Africa. I asked them how many of their students were living with HIV. 'None,' they replied confidently.

I pointed out that across their nation around 1 in 5 people of student age were living with HIV, so they could expect a similar proportion on campus to be so. HIV was therefore one of the most urgent challenges facing their university, with more students likely to become infected every month, yet they were not bothering to run any kind of prevention programme.

An African pastor and his wife came to dinner in our home. We asked about AIDS. The situation was not too bad, they said. But

'As a pastor I used to think AIDS was a problem in the community, but not in my church. So I was very shocked when 2 out of 9 of our leaders tested positive for HIV a few weeks ago, along with several other church members. Now we are doing all we can to help support those who are infected, and their families. We are also doing our best to stop the virus spreading.'

Pastor, Church of Christ, West Africa – January 2009

later they told us that her three brothers were all dead from AIDS, her father and mother also, and one of her sisters. Her other sister had tested positive for HIV and was becoming ill. Soon only she would be left. The pastor was taking AIDS funerals most weeks.

So we asked what he was teaching about HIV in the church. We expected that the church would be very active in its own ministry to people with HIV, and in community prevention, talking to their own young people and so on.

His face fell. 'Actually,' he told us, 'it is very difficult culturally to talk about. But we do have a programme for engaged couples. We insist they go and get tested and if one is infected, we refuse to marry them.' That was the extent of his church's response – in a nation that has strong AIDS programmes and where many other churches are very active.

He did not know how to change the situation, how to make a start, what he could do, and whether it would really make a difference. And his approach to engaged couples could land him in trouble later. (See page 70.)

We started to share stories about what other pastors had been doing in similar situations. How many lives they were saving. How it was affecting the whole mission of the church in a positive and powerful way. Their eyes lit up as they caught a vision of what could change. It was not impossible. Others were doing it. They were going to need more help, but they began praying and hoping for change that night.

Sharing the love of Jesus

When a church volunteer goes into a home – whether a rural African dwelling, an urban slum, a small apartment or a large house – that person carries the presence of Christ. Jesus has no body of his own: the church is his body. We are his hands, his feet, his smile, his voice, his heart and his touch.

The only part of God that people see could be the life of Jesus in you or me. As we go where the person is living, and give him a hug, bring her water or medicines, or food for her young children, or take his hand, we too are making a bit of history: a powerful declaration of God's love, a prophetic statement of his heart to people who often feel totally rejected by the church. The church cannot stay silent when faced with this issue.

That is why the World Health Organisation declared this obvious truth: 'The most effective way to prevent sexual transmission of HIV is to abstain, or for two uninfected individuals to be faithful to one another. Alternatively the correct use of a condom may reduce the risk significantly.'

In some countries up to a third of women with HIV have been celibate and then faithful, yet are sick and maybe dying because their husbands have HIV as a result of other relationships.

Time to help – easy to make a start

Compassionate care for the ill and dying, saving lives through prevention, and community development go hand in hand. Those involved in care often have the greatest credibility and impact. Then people see the reality of the illness and change behaviour. They are also stirred up to do all they can to help prevent further spread of HIV in their communities, to help the dying and orphans left behind. But changing behaviour can be hard when someone is hungry or homeless and takes risks every day by selling sex to survive.

Is your church or organisation prepared at leadership level for HIV? Any growing church may find people with HIV as members. If you don't think they are there, maybe look again. Remember members of your church may not even realise they have HIV.

Many pastors and priests across Africa and Asia are leading by example and being tested themselves, even if they do not feel there is a need to do so personally. They then encourage their congregations to do the same: going to the local clinic for personal counselling and

'I have encouraged people in my church to feel bad that people with HIV and AIDS are leaving our church. Now people who are infected are feeling loved. Some people invited to AIDS seminars are ashamed to come to the meeting, thinking that all those who are there are infected. The study of the Good Samaritan has remained a permanent calling to my life since the training programme I attended. We have started a series of meetings with the youth, most especially the young girls with the help of my wife. Next month I am inviting all the churches under my supervision together to make them aware of AIDS.'

Church of God pastor, West Africa – 2009

testing. Most large churches in hard-hit areas have been shocked to find that HIV has spread widely among their congregations. Of course these churches also need to tackle prejudice and stigma so that those within their communities who test positive are able to make themselves known and receive support without fear.

Many churches in countries like Ukraine and Russia are finding that members have HIV because of former drug-injecting lifestyles. These churches are now becoming involved in prevention as well as care.

ISAAC (International Substance Abuse and Addiction Coalition) is an international association of Christian drug rehabilitation programmes. The majority of residential drug rehabilitation centres in the world are in former Soviet bloc nations. Most are run by local churches – and most of those churches had little interest in HIV until their own people started to become unwell.

It costs nothing to be a friend or to speak about HIV

People with HIV are often very sensitive to other people's reactions, and we need to take time to listen to how they are feeling. We must help each person see that in the midst of great uncertainties, our own constant support and friendship is not in doubt, just as God's faithfulness and love is not in doubt.

People living with HIV may feel anxious or sad, or that life is not worth living, especially just after they receive a positive test result. They may feel rejected and think that nobody really cares or understands. Some people feel great anger about how they got HIV, or guilt about passing on the virus to others without realising. Feelings of isolation and loneliness may be intense. Fear of the process of dying is often far greater than the fear of death itself.

Stigma is a huge issue. Many church leaders in different parts of the world have been intolerant of those with HIV – so much so that people with HIV have felt that they had to leave the church once their situation became widely known. Thankfully attitudes are changing, but we have a long way to go.

The impact of HIV is also growing in India, China and other parts of Asia.

It costs nothing for pastors to preach about HIV, especially about the stigma that is still in our congregations and parishes. What it takes is courage to reach out to members of the church

'I have been stigmatising and discriminating [against] those affected with HIV and AIDS directly and indirectly, by not caring for them or giving them any support either physically or financially. I feel bad about my past actions and behaviour. I am really sorry. I will show them love and care in future. I will give them spiritual and physical help. I will never stigmatise those with AIDS again.'

First Baptist Church pastor, West Africa, 2009

who are HIV-positive, and ask them for advice on how to preach about stigma and rejection, since they often have first-hand experience of it.

People living with HIV may need simple practical help most of all, rather than just comforting words or a listening ear. Many want to counsel someone with HIV, but who is really prepared to do that extra little bit? People may need someone to accompany them to medical facilities, to provide food for their family, help cook a meal, help with laundry, help them to wash or dress, or help with school fees for their children.

And when life is over, the children remain. Some 15 million have been orphaned already. Who looks after them? And who is working to save the lives of the next generation of young parents? It is easy to focus on care and neglect prevention.

These kinds of things are what this book is about.

Praying for a people movement

Organisations, projects and buildings are not really the answer to HIV. A single project or hospital has very limited impact. The answer to HIV is a global people movement: when tens of millions more men and women become passionate about making a difference, not only going into the homes of those who need help, but also carrying a life-saving message of hope wherever they go. This is about mobilising entire villages, towns, cities and nations.

Governments are looking to the church for help

Large international development agencies and governments are looking to the church to respond. They recognise that in many places

where HIV is a serious problem, the strongest community organisations are churches, and that church leaders often have huge influence
in the community. They also see the passion, integrity and track
record of Christian hospitals and clinics over more than 100 years of
service in healthcare. And they also know that Christian hospitals, in
places like New York and Kampala, were often the only ones taking
care of people with AIDS at the start of the pandemic, showing more
compassion than many government hospitals.

They know that Christian agencies provide professional, excellent
care in many thousands of hospitals and clinics across many of the
poorest nations. They also see church commitment to health promotion, education, building schools and investing in young people,
over decades. But they also have concerns about our tendency to
judge others and about our paternal attitudes sometimes to those
in need.

Government leaders are often astonished at how church leaders
inspire millions of people to give time as volunteers, and the impact
on our communities with limited resources. They like our role models
and healthy messages. They admire our deep involvement in communities they find hard to reach – whether drug users, sex workers,
truck drivers, prisoners and so on. They are impressed with how
church leaders are able to help provoke entire communities to action,
encouraging people to change their attitudes and actions.

But these secular and government agencies now have a fresh
challenge to the Christian community. They say things like:

'Measure the impact of your HIV projects. Record the numbers
you help and the statistics about what you do. Show how you are
cost-effective and efficient. Prove to us you use money well. Show
us that parts of the church are able to reach into different parts of
the community, regardless of what connection they may have with
the church, including youth, orphans, pregnant women, drug users,
commercial sex workers and men who have sex with men. Tell us how
you can scale up your work to reach much larger numbers, without
loss of quality. Show us how 10 or 20 projects in an area can work
together across a region or city as part of a national programme. If
you can do these kinds of things, we have funds available now to help
you grow.'

You and I are part of God's answer

You and I are part of God's answer. The church is one of the largest community-based people movements on earth. Almost a third of the world's population would say that they are Christian – 2.1 billion people.[1] The church employs more people than any multinational organisation and influences more people than any government. It contains the world's largest resource of volunteers, and raises huge amounts of money. The church is beyond the control of any human leader, council, committee or government. It has branches and buildings in every part of the world, and members meet in tens of millions of homes. It is one of the world's biggest informal networks for passing on new ideas.

That is why agencies like UNAIDS and the World Health Organisation say that the church has an important role to play in the struggle against HIV, alongside other faith-based groups. So this book is not only about HIV and about what Christians can do to save lives and care for those affected, but also about how to do it all *better*, and to do it in partnership together, to have the greatest impact on our world, in the name of Jesus.

At the back of this book you will find two blank pages for you to list things you feel called to do in your own response to HIV.

Patrick Dixon
May 2010

---

[1] *World Christian Encyclopaedia*, 2001 Edition

CHAPTER ONE

THE RACE TO SAVE LIVES

After more than two decades in the global campaign to prevent the spread of HIV and treat AIDS, and more than 100 years of health promotion, the good news is that our world now knows a lot more about what works.

We know how to help save the lives of young people, older people, unborn babies and so on. We know how to improve the health of people with HIV. It does not cost a lot to teach someone how to stay safe and healthy. The most powerful prevention tool we have is the voice God gave us.

While the basic principles of prevention are clear, different groups may prefer a different emphasis in their work. Christians often prefer to talk about abstinence and faithfulness, while many secular educators prefer to talk about condoms and harm reduction.

So much time and effort has been wasted in a fight of words between some of those who support different approaches. We need to get on with the job of saving lives. Every day more people get HIV. Every part of the community has a role to play, even though we may emphasise different things. The former Director of UNAIDS, Dr Peter Piot, often said: 'All kinds of prevention efforts have value as part of an overall national strategy.'

Breaking the silence

When people start talking about HIV, what it is, how it spreads, about testing, treatment and how people can protect themselves, then infection slows down. When parents talk with their children, church leaders with their congregations, teachers with their pupils, office

27

workers with their peers, and villagers with their neighbours, then behaviour starts to change.

When people with HIV feel accepted and able to tell their own stories; when families are able to grieve openly for relatives who have died; then the message grows in power.

Churches often focus on care rather than prevention

Churches often begin by caring for their own members. But here is a key challenge: are you spending the same amount of time and money on prevention as you are on caring for those affected? It is short sighted and foolish to spend most of your HIV resources on care programmes when almost all future infections can be prevented.

The trouble is that the needs of those who are sick are immediate, desperate and often overwhelming – and can take up almost all our resources, as they knock on the doors of the church, our homes and our hearts. But if we don't stop new infections today, we will be even more overwhelmed tomorrow – even if there is better access to treatment.

Someone once told me with pride about the wonderful children's unit they had built to treat those with HIV in Southern Africa. It was beautiful and much better equipped than local hospitals. However, their expensive project could help only 100 children a year. With only a tiny fraction of their budget they could maybe prevent several thousand more children becoming infected with HIV every year.

So what is more important? To build a second unit for another 100 children a year, all of whom are sick or dying, or to save the lives of thousands of babies about to be born to mothers with HIV, or to educate many thousands of young people about HIV? Many Christian supporters in wealthy nations are willing to pour millions of dollars into care projects for children, but almost nothing into testing and prevention. Surely we should tackle the roots of the problem?

A key aim in *all* HIV programmes should be reduction of HIV transmission. You only have today to prevent someone's infection, but the next 10 to 20 years to plan their treatment and care. We must do all we can to respond effectively to this huge problem. Care and treatment programmes are vitally needed, but they are *no* answer on their own to the spread of HIV. Imagine what would happen if all Christian schools in the world took HIV seriously and gave accurate information about reducing its spread. The world would change!

Practical prevention based on common sense and experience of health promotion over many decades

We know from anti-smoking and other health promotion campaigns over many decades that people very rarely change their behaviour as a result of a single event. Behaviour tends to change across a whole nation as culture changes.

We have huge amounts of data, from many decades of work in many nations, on the impact of different health campaigns around the world. We can easily adapt these same general principles to HIV. We can:

- tell stories about people affected by the illness;
- mobilise the whole community in promoting healthy living: doctors, nurses, church leaders, influential people, youth workers, politicians, parents;
- get simple health messages across in every kind of media: TV, radio, posters, leaflets, newspapers, magazines, books, cinemas, street theatre;
- help people understand that the threat is real to them personally;
- give people choices and the confidence to make up their own minds;
- help people deal with peer group pressure – support people to change, and to help each other to do so;
- keep repeating health messages (every year you are speaking to new people and people forget all the details of your message anyway);
- take a very long-term view – changing a whole nation takes time.

Changing behaviour is always the *real* challenge. We know from decades of experience with other health issues that awareness campaigns alone have limited impact in changing behaviour. We have to go further.

So what does 'going further' mean when it comes to HIV prevention?

1. Focus effort for greatest impact

HIV prevention can be very effective when targeted at those most at risk. Often these are the most marginalised people in society – the very people Christians are called to serve. Examples within the ACET family have been men in drinking clubs and boda-boda (motorcycle taxi) drivers in Uganda, sex workers and truck drivers in India, those who inject drugs in Scotland, men who have sex with men in parts of Central Asia, and healthcare workers in Romania.

The key is to work hard to establish trust with informal members of the group you are targeting – for example training peer educators from the most affected communities to help spread key health messages. Targeted prevention often requires long-term investment for best results.

2. Adjust, adapt and change your messages to fit each audience

Your prevention message will depend on the situation. For example, what is the best message to use with a class of 11-year-old girls, with no previous sexual health education, in a strictly Muslim country? Or with engaged couples where one person in each couple is HIV-positive? Or in a church where use of condoms is regarded as sin even in marriage? Or with a group of sex workers who all have HIV, with children who are also HIV-positive, who want to continue as they are, intending to have sex that night with many different clients, charging different rates with and without condoms? Or with a group of injecting drug users who are about to share a single needle and syringe? Start by listening very carefully to your target group:

- What do they already know and understand? What do they need most from you?
- What is their culture, age, gender, situation?
- What are they most interested in and what do they most care about?
- What kind of risks are they becoming exposed to?
- Is HIV testing and treatment easily available? Do they feel comfortable about seeking help from those places?
- Are there specific issues in their culture/situation that you need to talk about?
- What pressures are they under from their peer group/culture, and how can you best build self-confidence?
- How can you best engage their interest, win trust, get across key messages and change how they think, feel and live?(Listen here to those influencing access to the target group, such as school teachers, prison governors, leaders of groups who inject drugs or of sex workers, church leaders and government officials.)
- What are they most concerned about?

- What do they want from you? How do they think you can best help?
- What will they allow you to do? When? Where? How often? For how long?
- What agreement do you need to make with them about what you will or will not do?
- Are they comfortable with the approach you are thinking of taking?
- Are *you* comfortable with what you are being asked to do – and does it fit with the culture and values of your church or organisation?

3. Follow up afterwards

It is important to find out how the programme is working. Ask questions.

- How did we do?
- Did you like and enjoy what we did?
- What was most helpful?
- Do you think it will change the choices you make in future?
- Did it change your attitudes to those of your friends or families or wider communities with HIV?
- Did you learn anything new?
- What could we do better next time?
- Would you like to help spread the message?

(See pages 168–174 for ways to help evaluate the impact of your prevention work.)

How much time with each group?

You may be able to work with the same group over weeks or months – especially if you are with them anyway as a teacher or youth worker, for example. Or you may only have time and access for a couple of sessions.

Most educators have many demands on their time and have to make difficult choices about the numbers of people they reach and the time they feel able to give to each group. Remember the example of Jesus. He made sure disciples were with him wherever he went. Those disciples would soon begin recruiting and helping more people become disciples. Jesus created a people movement of faith, which rapidly spread across the whole world.

Lessons learned in sharing HIV-prevention messages

We need to pay close attention to the following areas if we want maximum impact:

- Knowing and understanding all we can about the HIV epidemic in our community.
- Making sure we ourselves have a good understanding about HIV.
- Targeting our greatest efforts on those most at risk.
- Helping people understand the relevance to them personally.
- Encouraging people to be tested for HIV if they may have been exposed.
- Repeating messages in order to change people's behaviour.
- Understanding that community support is vital to reinforcing key messages.
- Taking HIV prevention out of heated political debates and just getting on with it.
- Understanding that motivated volunteers/church members can play a vitally important role.
- Forming partnerships between local churches and organisations in order to release new resources.
- Using simple, short, well-defined programmes that are quick and easy to reproduce and adapt.

But he also gave time to educating large groups, even though many of those attending would only ever hear him once. Both approaches are important: small groups and large.

So, for example, short school assemblies for up to 1,000 students at a time do reach huge numbers of students with basic information, but are likely to be far less effective than smaller groups where students can discuss and relate personally to what is being talked about.

Stages towards behaviour change

Always remember that behaviour change is a process. ACET Uganda has developed a three-stage approach:

1. Information

People must know the facts and what choices they have. Adapt the message to your audience. Fill in the gaps in the information available to them.

2. Identification

Help people explore whether they may already have been at risk or could be as a result of future decisions they make.

3. Interaction

Help people think through how they want to respond. Do they want to be tested for HIV? Offer life-skills training that enables people to reduce their risk of infection. This may include helping them to feel more confident about keeping to the decisions they have made and resisting peer pressure, enjoying long-term, fulfilling sexual relationships, taking personal responsibility for behaviour and respecting others.

ACET Uganda has found that HIV is best discussed as part of general sexual health education and wider issues. Peer groups are really helpful in encouraging people to live more safely. Life skills used to be passed from one generation to another, but this is happening less because of changes in society as people move from rural to urban areas. Churches are often very influential and can help build life skills in young people based on traditional culture and teachings.

But whatever HIV-prevention approach you take, whatever group you target, you will soon find yourself faced with big questions about what *messages* to give. That is what we will look at next, before looking at ways to reach very large numbers of people effectively.

CHAPTER TWO

WHAT HEALTH MESSAGES SHOULD WE GIVE?

So, then, prevention is vital and urgent. We want to do all we can to save lives. But what health messages should we give to those in our churches and in the wider community? In particular, what should we be saying about abstinence, faithfulness, condom use and other related issues? How should we vary the balance of our messages for different ages, cultures and situations? What are the most effective ways to prevent new HIV infection?

What is a balanced prevention message?

You may be a Pentecostal pastor in Central Africa who preaches from the Bible every week to a congregation of 5,000. You may be a government worker in Edinburgh in charge of condom distribution or needle exchanges. You may believe that everything you do and say must be based on what Jesus teaches as recorded in the Bible; that the traditional teachings of the church must be followed. Or you may not believe in God at all, and prefer to follow humanist values.

But whoever you are, whatever your beliefs, whatever your job, I believe we all have things to learn from each other to find answers to HIV.

This chart shows how a government/secular approach tends to differ from a church approach. Governments are learning from churches and churches are learning from governments.

Government and secular workers often think most about mechanical and medical answers to HIV. Many governments tend to put huge efforts into condom distribution, testing and treatment. They do not feel it is their role in society to tell people how to conduct their private lives. Pastors and church workers tend to think about relational and

Government Approach	Church Approach
Mechanical (condoms)	Relational (abstinence, marriage, faithfulness)
Medical (HIV testing, treatment)	Spiritual (pastoral, preaching, prayer)
When funds run out, programmes stop	Part of the church's calling to serve community – with volunteers
People and policies can change with every government	Church may have been active in a local community for decades

spiritual answers. Churches often put most of their efforts into teaching abstinence, marriage and faithfulness; into preaching God's standards; into pastoral support and prayer for the sick. But we all need each other.

UNAIDS has said: 'The condom is the single most effective tool we have to prevent the transmission of HIV.' However, many church leaders don't like talking about condoms as part of any health message from the church. They are often more comfortable talking about 'holy living' or testing for HIV.

The Bible encourages church leaders to talk about sexual behaviour and relationships

First, there is nothing new about church leaders talking about sexual health, behaviour and relationships. Moses was commanded by God to do so, and taught all his leaders to do the same as part of their healthcare system.

Moses was given power by God to heal leprosy – a dangerous and infectious illness at that time – for example in his sister Miriam (Numbers 12:10–15). Yet God also gave him health regulations about leprosy. The priests were required to teach about prevention (transmission, disinfection) and ways of testing for infection (physical signs). They were also responsible for preventing sexually transmitted infections (Leviticus 15).

Priests were not ashamed 3,500 years ago to talk about sexual behaviour in their congregations, and we should follow their example today. God gave them a holistic ministry. Teaching about healthy living was as much part of their ministry as teaching about holiness or praying for the sick.

Jesus also obeyed these laws. When Jesus healed a leper, he told the man not to talk publicly about it until the priests confirmed the healing (Matthew 8:1–4). We can also pray for healing, but we must make sure that anyone who thinks they have been healed is carefully checked out by the medical authorities. Priests may have been the local experts in health 3,500 years ago, but today they do not have the technology or training to confirm healings, unless they are medically qualified and working in a properly equipped healthcare centre. (See page 117 for more on healing.)

Many churches now include full sexual health education in their own faith-based schools. Such education has been shown to reduce numbers of unwanted pregnancies in teenage girls and sexually transmitted infections, including HIV, and it helps young people to have the confidence to make their own healthy lifestyle choices.

What is really going on in your church?

A big problem is unreality in the church. Pastors may hope that almost all their congregation are abstinent before marriage and faithful once married. However, surveys suggest that the sexual behaviour of church leaders in some countries may not be so different from that of their congregations, and the sexual behaviour of their congregations may not be so different from that in the wider community. The levels of HIV infection can be similar inside and outside the church, which is why the testing of church members is often as important as testing in the wider community.

Pastors have a God-given duty to discuss these things. It is easy to reply: 'In my culture we do not talk about sex.' That may have been true in the past, but it has to change in future. If we are silent and people die as a result in our churches, we will surely be judged by God as partly responsible.

Many things to do with sexuality can be hard for church leaders to talk about, especially with young people, but they need to understand how their own bodies work in order to be able to protect themselves. In some cultures many are quite ignorant about the mechanics of sex, and how different kinds of sexual behaviour can result in a higher or lower risk of HIV infection.

Church leaders often worry that discussing these kinds of things can actually encourage inappropriate sexual activity. This is usually a fear about corrupting the innocence of the young. But sadly the reality can be that their innocence has already been corrupted by relatives, friends, films, TV programmes or the internet. We may not realise what is happening and avoid vital issues where teenagers or children need help now – maybe at a much younger age than we might have planned for.

So at what age, and in what situations, should certain topics be first discussed? The answer, of course, will vary according to local culture and traditions.

Abstinence and faithfulness only?

Some Christian workers say that only abstinence and faithfulness should be taught in schools. They favour programmes like the *Silver Ring* pledge, and point to over 25,000 young people in America who have committed themselves to staying virgins until marriage, and to wearing a special ring to show this. Some 2.4 million have signed a similar *True Love Waits* pledge.

Those who promote abstinence point to surveys suggesting that teenage pregnancy rates fall significantly as a result of effective abstinence programmes, as does the age of first sexual experience and numbers of partners before marriage.

However, others reply that such 'narrow' messages may actually increase the spread of sexually transmitted infections if young people are not properly prepared when they end up taking risks (which some inevitably do). Although abstinence programmes may delay the age of first sexual activity, and young people who participate may have fewer partners before marriage, the same teenagers may also be less likely to use condoms when some of them inevitably do experiment in relationships. Some reports have also suggested that more of them will up experimenting with oral and anal sex, thinking it is not 'real sex' and so does not violate their pledge, and carries no risk.

There can be another problem with abstinence-only programmes. Many people have been abstinent before marriage and faithful since but have still got HIV through their partners, so prevention of sexual transmission of HIV is more complex than abstinence and faithfulness alone.

So what is the answer? How do we find the right way, but one that respects Christian, biblical values? How should we adjust our messages to suit our audience (10-year-old girls in a Sunday school class will require a different message from 23-year-old students in a local university)?

'ABC' approach has been popular with churches

Many church leaders, parents and teachers like the approach of the Ugandan government: **ABC** – **A**bstinence, **Be** faithful, Use a **C**ondom. ABC has been a popular, useful and easy to remember lesson plan for educators around the world, and is easy to promote in the media. It has been a useful starting point, but it does have limitations, especially as the nature of the epidemic changes.

Depending on who is in our audience, prevention messages may need to include other methods of transmission, such as sharing unsterile needles, or mother to baby.

We may need to cover other risks that are relevant in different cultures – for example, the traditional practice of passing on a widow to the brother of a man who has died. Inheriting widows is an ancient custom which is common in some African nations. The tradition has encouraged the spread of HIV in some parts of Africa, where husbands die of AIDS and their widows are themselves HIV-positive.

The practice of 'dry sex', where a woman places herbs inside her before intercourse to reduce natural lubrication, increases the risk of HIV transmission. But once men understand what causes vaginal lubrication, and how it increases naturally as part of a woman's desire for them, they often stop dry sex altogether.

Prevention approaches should also include the power of HIV testing to prevent spread, because this helps people to change their behaviour as a result, as well as access treatment. We also need to teach about how to reduce the risk of babies being born with HIV.

Which prevention methods work best?

Proving which prevention methods work best is very hard. Research would need to run for at least five years and include a large number of people from similar social, cultural, religious and ethnic backgrounds.

Ending wife inheritance in Kenya

Tom Onyango, 32, was forced to marry a second wife after his first wife died. Now he campaigns to end the custom of wife inheritance, which puts people at risk of contracting HIV.

The custom of wife inheritance means that if a wife dies, the widower is paid to take another wife from his in-laws. If a husband dies, the elders sit and choose another husband for the widow from their clan. The couple must have sexual intercourse, with one of the elders watching.

This practice puts people at increased risk of contracting the HIV virus, which is why the Movement of Men Against AIDS in Kenya (MMAAK) is campaigning to do something about it.

Tom is a volunteer for MMAAK. He comes from Kano/Angola, in the outskirts of Kisumu, where wife inheritance is a common occurrence. It often happens as a result of poverty and Tom is no exception. Tom's first wife became ill and tested HIV-positive. She died without telling Tom she had the virus – her sister told Tom several years later.

'Immediately after my wife's burial, the elders and my in-laws forced me to have a new wife, a relative of my late wife. I had to do it because of my culture, but I didn't like it at all,' says Tom.

This marriage was not happy. Eventually Tom's wife left and Tom was told to take a third wife. This time he refused and said he would only take a wife of his own choice. At this time, he discovered he was HIV-positive. He did not know when he had contracted the virus, but was aware that the wife inheritance practice was putting him and others at risk.

'I decided to take more control of my life. I went to a support group, where I met my current wife Lillian, who was also an HIV counsellor. Through my experience of wife inheritance, I didn't want others to go through it as well – it is quite common in this area and I wanted to help prevent it because it makes people very vulnerable to contracting HIV. I'm now working for MMAAK, championing a group of wife inheritors and group elders who discourage bad cultural practices like wife inheritance, early marriages and forced marriage.'

Source: CAFOD – www.cafod.org.uk

You can study a number of indicators that suggest you are making an impact, but it is almost impossible to *prove* one method is better than another. The official language has changed to '*evidence-informed*' rather than '*evidence-based*' methods. Even where you can show that a difference has been made, it is difficult to prove that all of that difference is the result of your own programme alone. We need to be humble about these things.

Condom programmes are easier to assess, because researchers

can look at local condom sales and how they change after an HIV-prevention programme. They can look at how many people who trade sex now use condoms with every client, or how many condoms are taken from machines in schools. But even then, it is very hard to prove how many condoms are actually used, or how well they are used.

How to assess if prevention works

We can use indirect methods to try to understand if a prevention programme works. For example, you can ask teachers for feedback on whether they think the lesson impacted their pupils. You can ask parents if your lessons provoked discussion at home. You can count the numbers in each youth group who come up afterwards to talk about getting a test for HIV. You can measure the number of pregnant women you have educated about HIV who have got tested, and the numbers of infected mothers you have treated with antivirals. You can count the number of sex workers who now say they are using condoms every time with their clients, or the number of drug users who have stopped sharing unsterile injecting equipment.

You can get students to fill in written surveys. You can ask if their attitudes have changed, or if they think they are likely to behave differently in future. You can repeat such surveys a few months later to try to discover what they actually did. However, you have to bear in mind that young people often do not tell the truth about their sexual activity, or use of illegal drugs.

It is usually much harder to assess the impact of HIV prevention than most people realise.

How to deal with national and local taboos in HIV work

In many countries there are taboos, traditions or strongly held beliefs that can accelerate the spread of HIV. In India and other parts of Asia many pastors have very negative attitudes to those with HIV. In Nigeria and Democratic Republic of Congo, many people in rural areas believe that AIDS-related illnesses are caused not by HIV but by a curse from a witch doctor. In parts of Uganda there were traditions of circumcising all young boys of a certain age with a common knife. In Kenya, other family members often inherit the widows of those who have died (from AIDS). Pastors need to take a close look at and analyse the situation in their own communities and speak out against practices that may spread HIV.

How to approach cultural issues:

- Understand fears and concerns – they are very real.
- Show deep respect for local traditions and culture, while also having the courage to challenge unhelpful or harmful practices.
- Win trust through providing practical help in other ways.
- Use someone who is respected as an authority by the other person to strengthen your argument.
- Present clear, simple facts – explain crisis and urgency.
- Continue to have conversations about these things until attitudes and understanding have changed.
- Offer a limited trial/experiment.
- Agree a modest first step.

Condoms can be part of the Christian answer to HIV

Traditions and cultures vary hugely, but the church can play a positive and active role in promoting the use of condoms to save lives in the context of wider health messages that include abstinence and faithfulness.

For Christians, there should be no reservations whatsoever about the use of a condom where the aim is to save the life of someone whose spouse has HIV.

We know from many studies that it is possible for a couple where one is HIV-positive and the other not, to have a sexual relationship for many years without infecting the other partner – when they use condoms carefully every time. But most churches recognise that condoms can also have a role to play in other situations.

Condoms can reduce risk of HIV infection by up to 95 per cent

Condoms without a doubt have saved millions of people's lives. Condoms also reduce the risk of many other sexually transmitted diseases, and cervical cancer, as well as being an important method of birth control.

While condoms offer good protection, they do sometimes fail, as we know from the fact that a few women in every hundred become pregnant each year, even when condoms are used every time they have sex. They may be damaged during use, as people fumble to put them on in the dark. They may be of poor quality, old stock or damaged by heat. Research shows that if used carefully, condoms can reduce the risk of HIV infection or of pregnancy by up to 95 per cent.

There are other practical challenges when it comes to condom use: for example, lack of access due to poverty and cultural issues.

Some 2 billion people exist on an income of less than $4 a day and a billion are experiencing hunger on a regular basis. The cost of condoms is a challenge in such nations. Very low-income countries cannot afford to provide them for everyone who needs them. Donors do not have the funds to provide enough of them, and hundreds of millions of people cannot afford to buy a new condom each time they have sex.

Therefore it is not realistic in such situations, nor sustainable, for government workers to give out messages that the answer for everyone at risk of HIV is for them to use condoms. As we have seen, prevention messages need to include other options that are appropriate to each person's situation.

Even where condoms are available and affordable, a major problem with condom use is that in many cultures a woman may risk a severe beating if she starts suggesting to her husband that they use a condom. And he may not be prepared even to think about suggesting it to his wife – as it could mean admitting that he has been unfaithful.

Smoking – a useful comparison

Discussing the issue of condoms with church leaders in Burundi, it was clear that they were very uneasy about the whole subject. Like many other evangelical and Catholic leaders in other parts of Africa, they thought that any mention of condoms to their congregations or young people would be encouraging them to do wrong things. Indeed, many of them had spoken out against condom messages that had been promoted by secular organisations or government departments.

I asked them if they approved of smoking. They said no. I pointed out that you can smoke cigarettes with or without filters, but filtered cigarettes are far safer. They kill fewer people. So if they had a friend who insisted on smoking, would they encourage them to smoke filtered cigarettes? Would they explain how much safer it was? Or would they feel it was just encouraging people to smoke even more? If they were the Minister of Health, would they approve a rule that only filtered cigarettes could be sold in shops?

They agreed that however much they were against smoking, the last thing they would want is for cigarettes to be even more danger-ous and they would agree that government advertising should explain that smokers are better off using filtered brands. I pointed out that the situation about recommending the use of condoms was similar. If someone is going to take a risk anyway, don't we have the same duty to warn them of the risks?

Paul Kabunga, Deputy Director of ACET Uganda, was speaking recently to a group of Nigerian pastors who were deeply troubled about condoms and Christian messages. They could not bring them-selves to talk about condoms at all with people, and thought such discussions were always morally wrong.

But they also knew that 10 per cent or more of the leadership teams and congregations in some of their churches were already living with HIV, with more people becoming infected every month.

Paul explained it like this: 'The church in Nigeria (as in other nations) teaches that sex before marriage is sin (fornication). Being unfaithful within marriage is sin (adultery). Fornication or adultery using a condom is also sin – but is much less likely to result in death from HIV. You are not encouraging people to sin by talking about condoms. You are not changing church teaching about abstinence or marriage. But you are saving lives.'

Those pastors also changed their minds, and recognised that condoms need to be part of a balanced Christian message to a community where many risks are being taken every day.

So how does HIV prevention work out in practice in a sensitive setting like high school? What is a Christian approach? Is it possible to reach large numbers of people in an effective way? We will look at this in the next chapter.

CHAPTER THREE

REACHING WHOLE COMMUNITIES

In many different parts of the world, churches have developed HIV-prevention programmes that have reached large populations. Here are some encouraging stories about what has worked well.

Why schools prevention work is such an urgent priority

Education at school about HIV, sexual health, addiction and related issues must be a number one priority. Young people are often most at risk. Many of them get HIV while they are high school age or shortly after. *There is no other way to reach most of an entire new generation of young people every year.*

In Uganda, very few young girls have HIV when they start high school, but until recently, 1 in 5 of them had got HIV by the time they were 15 years old. What a crisis if you are the head teacher of such a school! So, of course, going into schools has been a vital part of Uganda's HIV-prevention programme. Schools lessons on HIV and sexual health are one reason why infection rates among 15-year-old girls have fallen from 22 per cent to 7 per cent.

I am astonished at how some organisations neglect schools. They seem to think that HIV lessons in schools are not important, or that schools can manage on their own.

How else will we find young people? Walking the streets? At home?

'Why didn't they tell us more about HIV when we were all at school? Why didn't they spend time to talk with us about it? All they gave us was one short talk on sex by a teacher who was very embarrassed. If I had known then what I know now, maybe I would never have got HIV.'

We will miss millions this way or waste huge efforts – and even if we can find them, how can we persuade them to participate in HIV prevention? Yes, some people drop out of school, but school is still the *main* place in most countries where young people are organised to be together. Start there.

Schools are set up to educate, so adding HIV to a lesson or syllabus is easy, and low cost. Classes are organised. Students have to attend. Specialist educators can visit schools and spend time with students, while also training teachers so that HIV education becomes part of the culture of the school. Teachers have opportunities to follow up conversations, and quickly learn to teach HIV prevention themselves. Students are in the school for several years, so HIV issues can be covered in different ways as they get older.

Of course, a single one-hour lesson is unlikely to save many lives on its own. It needs to be part of a wider, ongoing school awareness campaign, or part of a national programme that includes radio, TV, leaflets, posters, community workers, parents, church leaders and so on. But it is very foolish and short-sighted to ignore opportunities to work with schools. Many young people may lose their lives as a result. So what action are you taking yourself?

How to reach high school students with HIV prevention

Here are things to consider when educating young people about sex and drugs. This approach is welcomed by the vast majority of church leaders, and is very popular in schools, whether in Africa, Asia, America; Western, Central or Eastern Europe; or Australasia. It is based on what we know works in every other area of health promotion; on experience over many decades in disease prevention. It is also based on the realities of daily life. Many millions of high school pupils have attended classes based on these common principles, run by many Christian agencies such as ACET, as well as by many secular agencies.

High school is an ideal place to work because so many young people attend, most parents and teachers want students to hear about healthy living, and the school organises everything for you. It is almost impossible to reach so many thousands of young people, so rapidly, at such low cost, in any other way.

Serving the school staff

Schools work is a very sensitive area, where people may have strong views on how sexual health and HIV prevention should be taught. This will vary between countries, regions, communities and schools.

A schools educator is there at the invitation of the teacher to be a servant to the school and a guest in the classroom. Topics to be covered, methods and general approach should all be agreed beforehand. Most schools in most nations are looking for the same things, but expressed in different culturally appropriate ways.

Whatever your views, whatever you prefer to teach, you will be limited to what the head teacher permits. And head teachers are hugely influenced by parents when it comes to how sexuality and drugs are talked about. That means being very sensitive to their culture, needs and situation, and guided by them.

Parents want helpful role models/teaching about relationships

Most parents are very concerned about risks to their children. It's the same in Africa, Europe, Latin America, Central Asia – or anywhere else. Parents want good role models in schools, and for their children to grow up confident enough to make their own healthy choices, to be happy, safe and have a long life. They want sexual health taught in the context of long-term relationships, family life, self-control and waiting for the right person (abstinence).

In my experience, head teachers in most high schools do expect condoms to be mentioned (and may insist on it), but *only* in this wider context. Actually pupils may not take you seriously if you don't mention condoms at all – they may already know far more than you realise. So talk about what they are thinking about. You risk being laughed at behind your back for being ignorant, naïve or too embarrassed to say what is true: that condoms can reduce the risk of HIV infection.

Young people often take sexual risks when they are drunk or under the influence of drugs, and forget all health messages. If they are intoxicated, they can also become careless in using condoms, even if they decide to use them. So it is really important to talk about alcohol and drug use as well as sexual behaviour – and maybe smoking tobacco too. Research shows that if young teenagers start smoking by the age of 13, they are more likely to abuse alcohol at a young age. Smoking

'We are still alive, yet we do not live any more'

This cry from the heart was received by ACET workers in Russia.

'I plead with you to publish my letter. I am 18 years old. My name is Olga. I was taken ill with AIDS two years ago. I am in hospital.

Why have you adults thrown us under a tank? Why have you disrupted us with sex, pornography and drugs? We were young children and our fathers offered us to others to bed. And our mothers received money for us, their children. It is you who are guilty in our illnesses and death!

You adults wanted "freedom", "relaxation" and "enjoyment". You approved pornography, wanted more money. You advocated "free relations", doing everything to satisfy your desires. But we are dying! We will never get to know real love; we will not have families; we will not have our own children.

We are still alive, yet we do not live any more. You stole our childhood and our future too. When I meet old people in the street, I have very strange feelings; I cannot even describe them. There is anger, wrath, fear, envy, helplessness and inability to change anything. Too late. We who are young and are dying do not know what real love is. We do not understand words like "shyness", "morality". The meaning of all these words has disappeared both from our schools and our life too.

You were taught their meaning then and that is why you can live 70, 80 and more years. But we will not live these years! We will die young! What for? Why? Four of my friends, who used to be my schoolmates, have died already. Youth lie in mortuaries. We are burying each other already.

Why have you not warned us of your "safe sex"? We want to live. We would rather work hard on a field, rather drive a tractor than cars of foreign makes and die of AIDS. HIV and syphilis have become as normal among us as flu.

We were children, we had no idea how babies are born. We thought that storks bring them. If only we could have stayed in this children's ignorance without knowing your abuse.

Nobody is going to take you to court on our behalf. You did not kill any of us with your own hands, after all. You were disrupting our lives gradually, bringing us up on your "pictures", your films. In schools you were talking us into how to do "it" safely in cellars and forced on us devastating films and magazines.

You have not stopped that yet. You are going on, destroying the lives of even younger children than we were. Have you not had enough? Has not there been enough sacrifice yet?

How grateful I would be now to someone who might have snatched the cigarette out of my hand, who would have snatched syringes away from me, who would have slapped my face for offering my body to others, who would have talked to me about all this danger. How little was needed to get me out from under the tank when it was possible still. Please help those who need your help now. Be open for those who are serving these young people.'

Olga, Krasnodar region, Russia, 2001

cannabis is also much more likely if young people are already used to smoking tobacco.

Checklist for schools workers

Here are some simple things to make your schools visits more successful:

- Listen carefully to teachers about what the school needs from you.
- Develop clear, simple, personal, accurate lesson plans that can be easily learned and given by volunteers, with stories that young people relate to easily.
- Remember that involvement in care helps build respect and credibility – it gives educators stories to tell, makes HIV more real to people and shows your compassion is real.
- Keep formal talks short and deal with the real issues people are facing.
- Focus not just on raising awareness and challenging prejudice, but on encouraging behaviour change.
- Always respect the views of your audience and spend time developing relationships and trust.
- Use simple questionnaires to test knowledge and assist learning – young people can fill them in during lessons and take them away.
- As well as adapting key messages to each age group and school, try using different teaching methods – such as group discussions and debates.
- Use different media to start discussion, such as video, slides and posters. Discover what works best in your culture, taking into account the limited resources you have.
- Remember that things like drama and creative workshops can be fun and effective, but require huge amounts of team time. Such things may be better to reach larger groups.
- Integrate HIV prevention with other life-skills issues.
- Think about training some senior pupils as peer educators to help spread the messages across the school, and to give support.
- Do exactly what has been agreed you will do.
- Be ready for some students who may wish to talk privately about personal issues at the end of the class session. Be very wise about what kind of conversation you are drawn into, especially if you are on your own with a young student of the opposite sex. Think

about who else you can bring in on a conversation in such a situation.

- Expect that some students may wish to find out about how they can be tested for HIV, confidentially.
- Always ask teachers to remain in class for (a) training in how to do a similar lesson themselves in future; (b) protection: the teacher will witness everything that is said and done, so no embarrassing stories can be invented by a student; (c) continuity:the teacher can reinforce key messages by referring back to what happened during the lesson; (d) assessment and accountability – the teacher can provide feedback and a formal review of the lesson.
- Take comments and suggestions seriously and always look to improve.
- Encourage teachers to let other schools know about your programme.

Be sensitive and well prepared

You may be shocked by what even very young children talk to each other about at school, learned maybe from older brothers or sisters or pupils, or from cinema or TV.

Sometimes it is necessary to begin some kinds of discussion at a younger age than you might have planned, certainly long before they reach high school, because those children have got hold of very alarming and completely untrue ideas about sex, and are asking direct questions about these things. You need to take a very sensitive approach, closely guided by the teachers and parents in each school.

In all things be guided by the school

Working in schools is a privilege and should not be used as a platform for promotion of personal beliefs without the formal approval of those whose guest you are. However, if in the context of religious or life-skills classes an educator is asked by a teacher or pupil to present a personal perspective – for example on the Christian hope of life after death – then that is a different matter, so long as it is presented as a personal view open to discussion and debate. Be guided in all things by the local school and the teachers. They will often give you far greater freedom than you might have imagined, especially of course if the school is run by the church.

Schools programmes often create demand for more regular youth clubs, HIV-awareness groups, peer-support groups and other after-school activities. Students can help run these with adult supervision, in consultation with local schools and in many cases supported and resourced by churches.

Schools programmes across entire nations

Small teams can cover entire nations – if they work in partnership with local churches and other organisations. For example, ACET Russia has trained over 350 volunteers and hundreds of church leaders.

They have trained teams covering schools in more than 90 towns and cities, as well as working in prisons, youth projects and drug rehabilitation programmes. They have just five small regional offices, with fewer than 10 paid staff, most of whom are part time. It works so well because most educators are supported by their own churches as youth workers. The project is 'owned' by over 100 different churches and their leaders, who see the work as part of their own mission.

ACET Russia has passed on the vision to Belarus, Kazakhstan, Tajikistan, Kyrgyzstan and Uzbekistan and other countries, and has trained workers in many other organisations, so the impact of prevention grows.

Volunteers can reach many thousands of students each year, providing valuable training and gaining feedback from the students. They need support and regular meetings, ideally once a year, for training, HIV updates and encouragement, and they work closely with local churches and will help support educator teams.

We will look more at volunteers and how to grow programmes rapidly in later chapters.

Simple programmes spread faster

The simpler your programme is, the easier it will be to train people. In 1988, ACET UK developed a national comprehensive sexual health education programme, using either one or two lesson plans, each of which lasts up to an hour. These are adapted easily to a wide range of age groups and school cultures, and became the basis for the Russian programme above.

This programme includes a simple questionnaire that pupils can fill in and take away, which covers basic facts about HIV. Lessons contain informal discussions on HIV issues and the choices people can make. There is a focus on building up self-esteem and encouraging young people to have confidence in their own decisions.

Teachers like external educators coming in because students are often more open and relaxed when talking about these important issues with outsiders.

Teachers can use additional classroom materials for their own lessons for the other 40 weeks of the school year. (See www. acet-international.org for examples of lesson plans and other resources.)

How to reach a nation in 18 months

The fastest way to reach huge numbers of people in prevention or care is to train a lot of people – either volunteers or workers – funded by other organisations. And the fastest way to train a lot of people is to train other trainers, who in turn will train more trainers, to train yet others.

In 1989 Communism ended in Romania and within weeks a tragedy was revealed: tens of thousands of adults and children (mainly in state orphanages) had been infected with HIV through dangerous medical practices, which were continuing every day. The new government was in a race against time to reach every doctor and nurse in the country with an urgent message to stop these treatments. They asked ACET UK for help, in partnership with UNICEF.

Within 18 months the entire medical and nursing profession was reached, and the danger removed. The approach was simple. ACET leaders held a first HIV-prevention conference in Bucharest, with 50 senior doctors and nurses. Half of the conference was spent preparing these 50 people in small groups to organise the next five conferences on their own in different regions.

These regional conferences were held a few weeks later, with ACET UK team members taking part in each one. At each of these next five conferences once again a health message was combined with planning to organise five more. A few weeks further on, there were 20 to 30 conferences across the nation, which in turn gave rise to more. In less than two years, every doctor and nurse had been trained – at very low cost, and requiring very little input from ACET, compared to the impact.

The foundations of all effective training are similar to those for HIV prevention (listed on page 53). For example, we should start by learning about the needs of our audience, why they are there, what they want to learn, what they already understand, what they want to do at the end of the programme – and adapt.

Training pastors to mobilise thousands of people

Here is another example of a 'train the trainer' programme, this time
in Nigeria. In June 2008, 20 pastors attended a week long training
programme in a remote rural area in the middle of the country.Each
pastor committed themselves to training others and mobilising their
entire network. Within six months one pastor alone had succeeded
in reaching over 16,000 people in small and large groups, by training
groups of leaders who then took the message to others, who in turn
started new support and prevention groups, schools teams and so on.
He was helped with supplies of training materials and other resources.

Where to find training and prevention resources

Training resources are really important, but please, please do NOT
develop your own training resources, manuals, syllabuses, PowerPoint
presentations or anything else without first checking what others have
already done. Of course you will need to adapt materials and methods
to your own situation, but life is too short and resources are too scarce
to waste in 'reinventing the wheel'.

Huge amounts of leadership time are wasted every year by people
developing new resources – maybe to train home-care volunteers, or
pastors, or children's workers, or schools workers.

Contact projects that are doing similar work – preferably in your
own part of the world. Find out what materials they use and copy or
adapt them. Always give credit where credit is due and acknowledge
every source.

All training materials should be copyright free

Sometimes I come across wonderful training materials, which are
world-class, have taken a huge amount of time to develop and have
been well tested in the field. But they are not available to other
organisations. What a terrible waste of God-given time and effort.

That's why I am so glad that over a million chapters of *The Truth
about AIDS* have been downloaded online free of charge, and why I
am so glad that over 350,000 copies of the book you are now reading
have already been given away, or sold only at the actual cost of
printing, with free permission to use and adapt however people like.

I can understand project leaders saying they cannot provide copies

Training for different purposes – with common methods

You may be training laboratory workers or schools educators, pastors or teachers, theological students or home care assistants – but most principles are the same and easily adapted:

- Select key people to work with – your most important resource. What is your ideal participant and why? How will you find them? Could they be pastors of churches of more than 200 people, who also have influence over several other churches. It could be that such pastors are easily contacted through existing church networks, or by other leaders who attended previous programmes.
- Be clear about your purpose and ask each trainee what they want to achieve following the training.
- Find out early on what they already know so no time is wasted repeating things. If necessary, split the group into two or more sub-groups so training can be adjusted to the levels of participants.
- Focus on the basic skills needed to carry out an activity once trained, then ensure all who qualify achieve these.
- People have very busy lives, so keep training as short as possible. This also cuts costs.
- If possible, make sure your courses are approved by a higher authority (for example, by an educational institute), to give credibility and help ensure high quality.
- Give personally signed certificates to those who complete training, so that their personal credibility grows, and as a way of honouring those who are becoming involved.
- Develop excellent teaching materials that participants can keep, so that standards are kept to the same high level on every programme.
- New trainees should be supervised by experienced workers when they start.
- Remember that personal encouragement is important, through coaching, mentoring and discipleship.
- Involve participants in discussions, so that their own thinking has a chance to develop. Don't just lecture them.
- Use communication aids – such as posters, questionnaires and PowerPoint presentations with many photos or video clips – to get key messages across.
- At the end of training, ask each person to list the actions they intend to take over the next few weeks, to turn their hopes at the start of the programme into a reality.
- Follow up each trainee within a few weeks, to ensure that progress is really being made with their own specific objectives.
- Go on contacting them at regular intervals to monitor progress.
- Get each trainee to complete an evaluation form, giving their feedback at the end of the training, so that the programme can be improved.

(Adapted from ACET Nigeria, ACET Ukraine and ACET Russia)

of material for free. Sure, charge if you need to, but only for the actual costs of production, postage and packaging. Please don't try to make a profit on it. And remember that resources are very cheap if you produce in bulk. The more copies you can distribute, the lower the cost of each copy. For example, if many thousand copies are ordered at a time, to be printed in India, three copies will cost one US dollar. Production and distribution of great HIV resources could become a key part of your ministry. It can be a project in its own right. You will find many donors want to fund such work because they know how important it is.

Some projects say they need to make money from materials in order to pay the salaries of those who generate them, but this is not quite true, since their materials have already been written, so the only future costs will be production. Other projects say they want to fund their own work by making profits on materials to fund future work – so they are taking money from one HIV project to help another. What is the point in that?

Some project leaders are afraid that people will 'steal' all their ideas and work. But that is the whole idea. Imitation is the best form of praise. I can think of nothing more exciting than a million people taking ideas you have developed to save lives or better care for people with HIV, and turning them into new and better projects around the world. Anyway – who paid for the work? Those who fund your

AIDS association in India helps create training materials

Christian AIDS/HIV National Alliance (CANA) began as a network of Christian programmes involved in AIDS in 1997.

CANA encourages faith-based organisations to get involved in advocacy, communication, children at risk of HIV infections, value-based education, as well as focusing on community- and congregation-based AIDS-prevention and care efforts.

There is a major gap in the needs of those affected by HIV and the responses of the church and church-based agencies. There is a need for a comprehensive and integrated community-based approach.

Part of the mission of CANA is to help distribute useful materials to our member agencies and wider communities. As part of this we have been involved in publishing and distributing the *AIDS and You* book in English (an Indian version) as well as a Hindi version of this book, widely distributed across the CANA partners, pastors, evangelists and youth.

Christian AIDS National Alliance (CANA): www.cana-india.org

programme? So if the materials belong to anyone, you could say that they belong to your donors!

So then, let others freely use and adapt what you have produced. Publish it on a website. Let people download electronic versions of your resource files so they can easily make changes. But always insist that they give proper acknowledgement to your project, give the source of their materials, and explain how people can get copies of the originals.

And also ask them to email you the electronic files of any new versions they make, including translations. You can then add them to the list of free downloads.

The materials we need do not exist

Some people say that the training materials they need do not exist. If you feel this is the case, start by finding a programme as similar as possible to the one you are planning. If you find they have not yet written down their methods, ask them to record their next training sessions for you (audio or video) and send you a copy. Projects are often short of cash, so encourage them by paying for the costs of this. That means your own trainees can benefit immediately from the experience of other projects.

People often tell me that they have searched without success to find what they need. This lack of success is usually down to being poorly networked – they just do not have enough contacts. If this is your situation, talk to people who know other people. Search online, using engines like Google. Go to websites of agencies like Tearfund, Samaritan's Purse or UNAIDS. Materials may exist but may need translating into the appropriate language.

I remember being asked by Tearfund to help a group of churches in India write an AIDS care manual. They flew a number of us from different nations into the country and sent us around different regions. Before we went I said I was certain, even then in 1996, that we would find not just one, but several really good AIDS care manuals already published in India. And this indeed turned out to be the case. It showed us all that the real need was not to create new materials, but to improve communication between Christian programmes that were all involved in similar work in a nation of 1.3 billion people. As a result, CANA was born (Christian AIDS National Alliance). PACANET exists in a similar role to network across African nations.

Ways to prevent HIV spreading among injecting drug users

In many countries there is a big challenge to stop the spread of HIV among drug users who share needles. Spread can happen very fast. What can be done? This touches on many sensitive and controversial issues.

The most important thing is to have community workers who are in touch with drug users on a daily or weekly basis, to help support them and their families and provide advice on staying healthy.

They can also offer access to programmes to help them stop drug taking if they wish to do so. Churches play a leading role around the world in drug rehabilitation.

In some countries, governments run special programmes that provide alternative drugs so they can stop injecting.

However, many drug users may choose to continue to inject and not accept offers of treatment or rehabilitation. What then? Needle exchange programmes can reduce HIV transmission, as shown in many different studies of work with those who inject drugs. Drug users often share equipment because they do not have any of their own or it is worn out. Needle exchanges offer each drug user a new needle and syringe in exchange for their old ones.

However, many church leaders worry that 'harm-reduction' programmes like this one fail to tackle underlying issues and may appear to encourage certain lifestyles. They may be very unhappy about needle exchanges, for example; indeed their concerns may be shared by some national governments.

We should be slow to judge projects that take a different view from our own. We need to really understand the situations that project workers face every day in the lives of those they are seeking to save from infection. We also need to look at the evidence to see how these different approaches actually work.

Practical caring: painful and very upsetting choices

Christians are often presented with really hard choices in their daily HIV work. I remember driving with some ACET workers onto a large housing estate in the UK in an unmarked van (anonymity was essential, otherwise our clients might be attacked).

As we climbed out of the van, men and women, all drug users, appeared one by one from staircases and alleyways. They were mostly sleeping in rough conditions, some sharing floor space in various damp apartments. They were unknown to government workers or local hospitals, living in a shadowy world. But the volunteers I was with had found them, won their trust and were trying to support them.

We knew that some had HIV, but most had not been tested. Money was a huge problem for them. Some of them needed more than $200 a day to buy enough drugs to avoid slipping into withdrawal, which is really unpleasant, making them feel very ill and desperate. We discovered that they had only one dirty needle and syringe between them all.

More of the group could get HIV or hepatitis C in the next couple of hours through sharing that needle and syringe. But what could we do? What were our options? Do nothing, leave immediately and just start planning back at the office to look after many more people living with HIV? Teach them about how to sterilise that needle and syringe with diluted bleach before passing it on? Give each person their own clean needle, and agree to replace each blunt needle with one clean one on a regular exchange basis?

HIV is a development issue

Finally, remember that HIV is an issue of development. As we have seen, just focusing on HIV will not in itself halt it. Ignorance, lack of healthcare, poor communication, destitution, addiction, children earning money or food from sex; all these increase the risk. These cycles of deprivation need to be broken together.

Take, for example, a woman who provides sexual favours in return for money, food, medicines, illegal drugs or other things: how is she to live if she stops providing her services to men? Who will feed her children? Who will pay for her medicines? Prevention campaigns are not enough. We need a holistic approach.

And it is also wrong to assume that she will choose a different way to earn money if one is offered. Many sex workers find such attitudes among Christian 'rescue' missions very offensive and patronising.

Microfinance, income-generation schemes and other self-help programmes have a vital role to play, not only in raising general income in a nation, but also in helping those with HIV rebuild their lives and helping orphans survive.

Economic growth also provides taxes for governments, which means they can provide better health promotion and care.

One thing is certain: once you start talking about HIV, you will soon get asked a lot of questions. Here are some common ones, and some answers.

CHAPTER FOUR

QUESTIONS PEOPLE ASK

Wherever I go, many of the questions are the same. Things like: what is AIDS? Where did HIV come from? What about testing? When will there be a cure? Is breast-feeding safe for my baby if I have HIV? How can I stay well with HIV for as long as possible?

What is the cause of AIDS?

AIDS is caused by a virus called HIV. Your body is usually very good at destroying germs – bacteria, viruses, fungi or parasites. Its natural defence is your own immune system. HIV weakens your immune system so that other germs can invade and kill you.

When your immune defences are badly damaged, we say you are suffering from a deficiency of your immune system or an 'immuno-deficiency'. Some people are born with poor immune systems and others acquire a deficiency because of a disease. Because HIV is 'acquired' through an infection, we call it the Acquired Immunodeficiency Syndrome (AIDS for short).

HIV stands for Human Immunodeficiency Virus, which is the scientific name for the virus that causes AIDS.

It takes many years between being infected with HIV (where a person appears healthy but is infectious), developing early symptoms of AIDS, and then progressing finally to more severe illness or death. It is totally impossible to tell by appearances who has HIV. Antiviral treatment can slow down each stage of the process and lengthen life by many years.

Where did HIV first come from?

No one is certain where HIV first came from. Many scientists believe that HIV has existed for many decades, and may have developed from similar kinds of viruses in animals. There is no reason to look for blame. HIV infection in humans started somewhere and it is no one's fault.

As Paul Kabunga, who leads the ACET Africa region, often says: 'In my country when you see a snake around your feet, you do not stop to have a debate about where it came from. You kill the snake! Too many people waste time and effort in great debates about things like where HIV came from, when they should be saving lives.'

How does HIV spread?

HIV crosses between sexes and between people of the same sex when they have sex together, although it is far easier for the virus to spread between men who have sex with men than between women who have sex with women. (Same-sex activity is more common than many people think in places like sub-Saharan Africa.) The virus also spreads when blood or secretions from one person enter the blood stream of another, or through the womb, or from a mother's breast milk.

How can I avoid HIV?

If you know you are not carrying the virus, you will want to stay that way. You may want to make the decision, if you have not already done so, that the next person you have sex with will be the person you are committed to making love to for the rest of your life. But what if that person has had several partners before? What if your partner is unfaithful or is injecting drugs? Now that effective treatment is becoming more widely available, it is even more important to know your HIV status if you have been at risk, and for your partner also to know his or her HIV status.

If either of you is living with HIV, then it is very important to protect your partner's health by using a condom when having sex.

If you are in the medical or caring professions, you should already have clear instructions on how to protect yourself while also giving excellent care. The basic rule is to keep other people's blood and any other body fluids off your skin as far as possible.

My boyfriend says that I don't love him because I don't want to have sex with him

One thing is absolutely certain: he doesn't love *you,* or if he does, he doesn't respect you. If he is pressurising you to give yourself to him with no real commitment on his part, he is more interested in getting pleasure for himself than in building a relationship with you.

I know my boyfriend and he says he's a virgin too, so it must be safe

A man will tell you anything you want to hear in order to have sex with you, if he wants it enough. The world is full of hurt girls and women who have been badly let down and now have HIV as well. They agreed to have sex out of fear that the relationship would break up, or because he promised that they would get married one day. But he may have had no intention whatsoever of getting 'trapped for life'. You may be looking for a home and a husband who will love you, care for you and be a good dad to your children. But your boyfriend may just be looking for a good time.

Anyway, even if he is a virgin now, do you really think that he is never going to sleep with any other girl for the rest of his life? If he is so keen to have sex with you now before any commitment in marriage, he may be just as likely to try it out with someone else later on, maybe even after he has married you.

What happens when HIV enters the body?

HIV attaches itself to the white blood cells that help our bodies to fight off infection and stay healthy. These white blood cells normally float around in the blood, or get carried between the tissues of our body, searching out and destroying germs. There are hundreds of different germs and each kind of white cell is designed to attack one kind of germ. When white cells are infected with HIV, they forget how to fight infection, and learn how to make new viruses instead.

Why do you get ill with HIV?

Only certain kinds of white blood cells get attacked by the virus, but as they get fewer it gets harder for your body to kill certain bacteria and fungi. Most common germs are quickly destroyed, but one or two just keep on growing. The result may be a chest infection, TB or other illnesses such as thrush – often seen as a white coating in the mouth. After a while the body is weakened and other infections start to take over.

Some of these new infections simply cause you to feel run down or to lose weight, but the chest infections can kill and can be very hard to treat. Those who die of illnesses related to AIDS, do so mainly because of the other infections that take over the body when their immune defences are damaged, or from cancers related to HIV. TB is a very common cause of death in people with advanced HIV. Medicines for TB normally have to be taken regularly for many months, but in people who also have HIV, the treatment for TB can take longer.

HIV is a virus, but what is a virus?

A virus is a very, very small infectious agent (about 1/100th of a bacterium). A virus contains a piece of genetic code that teaches cells in your body how to make more viruses. This is like the genetic code that makes your hair brown, your nose and your ears the shape they are. Everything inside you is programmed by these genes, and amazingly almost every cell in your body has inside it all the instructions to make a complete copy of you.

What is the treatment for HIV infection?

Today's antiviral treatments can be very effective. They can keep people well for many years, but they cannot cure people. The medicines have to be taken for life and they must be taken correctly and regularly, following medical advice.

Manufacturers, governments and development agencies have taken steps to provide the drugs at much lower cost, working with Global Fund, UNAIDS and the World Health Organisation. But for most poor people, they are still far too costly – and if they are free, they are often unavailable.

In parts of Africa and Asia, people may go to get free antivirals, only to be charged for the other parts of their treatment or for tests, so they cannot afford to go again.

People who test positive for HIV should be offered free treatment with more than one kind of antiviral.

Choose to Care initiative – antiretroviral therapy

Each treatment programme employs a physician, professional nurse and project co-ordinator. After nurses and physicians have been trained, drug literacy courses are offered to home-based caregivers, to other medical staff and to patients themselves. In order to avoid unnecessary delays and to facilitate speedy delivery of services and medications, each site employs the same procedures:

- Home-based caregivers identify patients who meet a number of criteria; and arrange for the patient to receive a blood test at the therapy centre.
- Physician and nurse send blood samples to a laboratory in Johannesburg for CD4 count, viral load and full blood count.
- Sites are informed of results by email.
- Adult patients with CD4 counts below a certain level begin antiretroviral medication.
- Medications are pre-packaged for each patient.

Before beginning antiretroviral therapy, each patient must undergo training to encourage them to take medicines regularly, and treatment for other infections associated with HIV.

A faith-based response to HIV in Southern Africa: the Choose to Care initiative, UNAIDS best practice collection

Globally, less than one person in five at risk of HIV has access to basic HIV-prevention services. UNAIDS, WHO and UNICEF are working with governments around the world to help provide universal access to HIV prevention, treatment and care.

What about a vaccine?

Vaccines are our only defence against viral diseases. Polio, whooping cough, measles and other illnesses are rare now thanks to vaccines. A worldwide programme against smallpox has wiped it off the face of the earth. So why not HIV?

A vaccine encourages our bodies to develop special antibodies to get rid of a particular infection. The trouble with HIV is that the virus keeps changing its shape, making it very difficult to develop a vaccine. There are other viruses that change shape as well – such as flu and the common cold. But HIV changes shape faster than these.

We are many years away from an effective vaccine against HIV.

How can we stop HIV passing from mother to baby?

Sadly, several hundred thousand babies are born with HIV each year.

HIV can pass from the mother to her unborn baby during pregnancy or delivery, and it can also be transferred to the baby by the mother's breast milk. This is usually called mother to child transmission of HIV (MTCT). A range of different things can be done to prevent this, so it is important to make sure that all pregnant women have an HIV test.

If a pregnant woman tests positive for HIV, first the doctors check to see if she needs antiviral treatment herself. If she does need treatment, then this is a very good way to make sure that her baby will not get HIV. If she does not need antiviral treatment herself, the mother will need to have antiviral therapy during pregnancy and delivery to try to prevent HIV from being passed to the baby.

The antiviral drugs used to prevent transmission usually contain Nevirapine or Zidovudine (often called AZT). Using only Nevirapine may be the only option when women come very late for pregnancy care, but is not the best option to prevent transmission. In most high-income countries the rate of transmission of HIV to babies has been reduced to less than 1 per cent by using a range of medicine and good care for the mother during pregnancy.[1] Antiviral drugs should only be taken under medical supervision

Once the baby is born, the mother needs to consider whether replacement feeding — e.g. mother's milk substitutes — is safe, practical, affordable and acceptable long term. If it is not, she needs to breastfeed without *any* replacement feeds until replacement feeding becomes possible.

All mothers need access to clear information, support and counselling when making these difficult choices. (For more, see question on breast-feeding on page 65.)

How long should mothers with HIV be treated with antivirals?

Drug supplies are limited in some countries, so there may be very hard choices to make about how many people are treated and for how long. Until antivirals become more widely available, perhaps one answer is

---

[1] UNAIDS Fast Facts

to give only 14 days' treatment to each pregnant woman just before birth, and then a single dose at birth for the baby.

Other treatment centres may decide that all who start antiviral treatment should continue on it for the rest of their lives – but that may mean far fewer pregnant mothers can receive a short course of treatment, and could mean more babies are born with HIV. These are agonising decisions.

But there is more to healthcare than HIV! Imagine that an adult is sick with HIV in a country like Sierra Leone, in a remote village where young children die every week because the water is polluted by sewage or because there is no treatment for malaria or anything else, where the nearest clinic is 20 miles away, walking through the bush. Health planners in such situations have to look at the health needs of the whole community, as they decide what to do with their budgets.

We need to ensure that each programme makes the best use of limited resources in each local situation, and that the whole community is involved in such decisions. For example, a country with a very small health budget may have to choose between providing free antivirals for more people or providing other basic essentials such as gloves for surgeons and midwives. It is important that funds allocated to one purpose are not used for another (see pages 189–191).

Antiviral issues to consider

- Supply – are they really going to be available long term? If not, resistance may grow fast.
- Compliance – is the person really going to take antivirals regularly? It is vital the person takes medication every day to prevent the virus from becoming resistant.
- Monitoring – are facilities available for regular blood tests and for supervision? Antivirals can kill if they are not properly monitored.

What are the risks of breast-feeding if a mother has HIV?

During the first six months of a child's life, breast milk alone is the ideal food. It contains all the nutrients and water needed for healthy growth. It also provides good protection against many common infections. Replacement feeding should only be used if the mother has a safe water supply, sufficient income to buy replacement milk and can mix it correctly and hygienically.

Breast milk continues to be an important source of nutrients until a child is around two years old. However, after six months of age, all babies need increasing amounts of additional foods, called complementary foods, before eventually changing to family foods alone. Without a good mixture of these additional foods, babies will fail to grow properly.

Mothers with HIV have a difficult choice, as HIV can be passed on to the baby by breast-feeding. However, if the baby is fed only breast milk for six months, with no other liquid or food at all, and the mother then stops breast-feeding as quickly as possible, the risk is small.

Mixing breast-feeding with other kinds of food in the first six months of life can increase the risk of HIV in breast milk infecting the baby.

Research suggests that for every child dying from HIV through breast-feeding, many more die because they are not breast-fed. If babies are bottle-fed in poor conditions, where it is difficult to sterilise bottles and water, they are many times more likely than breast-fed babies to die from diarrhoea, pneumonia or other causes.

The longer breast-feeding continues, the greater the risk of HIV-infected mothers passing on the HIV virus to their babies.

- One in every 20 uninfected babies will become infected if breast-fed for six months.
- Two in every 20 will become infected if breast-fed for a year.
- Three in every 20 will become infected if breast-feeding continues for two years.[2]

What are the tests for HIV?

There are three main types of HIV test. You cannot tell from symptoms alone whether you have HIV.

The first type of test is the HIV *antibody test*. This test is most commonly used and shows whether a person has been infected with HIV. There are only two exceptions to this rule. First, babies born to positive mothers keep their mother's antibodies for up to 18 months,

---

[2] Text of this answer from *PILLARS Guide on Healthy Eating*, Tearfund. Statistics from London School of Hygiene and Tropical Medicine

so will test positive even if they turn out to be uninfected. Secondly, some people who have taken part in HIV vaccine trials may have HIV antibodies even if they are not infected with the virus.

Most people develop detectable HIV antibodies within six to 12 weeks of infection. In very rare cases, it can take up to six months. Getting tested earlier than three months after possible infection may result in an unclear test result, as an infected person may not yet have developed antibodies to HIV. The time between infection and the development of antibodies is called the 'window period'. During the window period people infected with HIV will not yet have antibodies in their blood that can be detected by an HIV test. Someone can transmit HIV to another person during the window period even though they do not test positive on an antibody test.

The second type of test is an *antigen test*. Antigens are the substances found on a foreign body or germ that trigger the production of antibodies in the body. The antigen on HIV that most commonly provokes an antibody response is the protein P24. P24 antigen tests are sometimes used to screen donated blood, but they can also be used for testing for HIV in individuals, as they can detect HIV earlier than standard antibody tests. Some modern HIV tests combine P24 and other antigen tests with standard antibody tests to enable earlier and more accurate HIV detection.

The third type of test is a *PCR test* (Polymerase Chain Reaction test). PCR tests detect the genetic material of HIV itself, and can identify HIV in the blood within two or three weeks of infection. PCR tests can be used for babies born to HIV-positive mothers, who retain their mother's antibodies for many months. They are rarely used to test for HIV in adults, as they are very expensive and more complicated to use than a standard antibody or P24 test.[3]

My baby has tested positive for HIV – is she infected?

The usual test for HIV does not work correctly in a newborn baby. This is because every newborn baby of a mother who has HIV will receive antibodies from the mother in its own blood while it is in the womb. That is why all such babies test positive for HIV, whether or not they

---

[3] Text of this answer is from Avert

are actually infected themselves. When you test around a year after birth, most babies turn out to be uninfected, even without treatment.

How can I stay healthy if I have HIV?

Anything that strengthens your immune defences is going to help keep you healthy, and things that weaken you should be avoided. Common sense tells you to take care of yourself. Eat proper regular meals, take some exercise, keep your weight reasonable, eat plenty of fresh fruit, cut out smoking (if you can without too much stress), cut down on alcohol, stop all other recreational drugs and make sure you get enough sleep. These low-cost measures are likely to prolong the life and well-being of most people and especially of those with HIV or early HIV infection. But don't waste money on 'cures' that have not been scientifically tested. And don't stop taking medicines from the hospital or clinic without discussing it with your doctor or nurse.

ACET clinics in India have seen remarkable results in caring for people with HIV with simple things such as better nutrition and vitamin supplements, a basic antibiotic to help guard against chest infections, plus an antifungal to protect against thrush. These approaches are becoming widely used, because they are low cost, effective and easy to provide safely.

Be kind to yourself. You may find it takes a long time to come to terms with the news. You will need a lot of support and encouragement from friends and family. Make sure you get enough rest. Slow down a little if you are getting more tired – and remember even coping with the news can be emotionally tiring.

Do all you can to avoid exposing yourself to more infections – whether to more HIV, to other sexually transmitted diseases or to other things. Make sure you register with the local hospital or clinic, so they can give you the best treatments they have available. Be very careful to take all medicines exactly as they say, and on time. If you feel unwell, seek help quickly and do not just hope it will all go away.

Think and pray about your longer-term plans. What is important to you? Are there any decisions you need to make? Take care not to jump into decisions you may regret without talking to others and waiting a while.

INERELA+
a network of 3,500 religious leaders with HIV

INERELA+ is an international, interfaith network of religious leaders – both lay and ordained, women and men – living with or personally affected by HIV. It is recognised that religious leaders have a unique authority that plays a central role in providing moral and ethical guidance within their communities; indeed their public opinions can influence entire nations. INERELA+ looks to empower its members to use their positions of respect within their faith communities in a way that breaks silence, challenges stigma and provides delivery of evidenced-informed prevention, care and treatment services.

The idea for this network was first publicly discussed in 2006 as a global expansion of ANERELA+, the African network. It was launched two years later at the 2008 International AIDS Conference in Mexico City. Before the founding of ANERELA+ in 2003, very few religious leaders in Africa lived openly with HIV nor were they willing to be open about HIV+ family members. The few that did had no support structure and no united voice. In all but the most accepting of communities, religious leaders usually kept silent for fear of stigma and discrimination. ANERELA+ sought to address these issues.

In just under five years, the two networks have grown to encompass over 3,500 members across five continents. It is hoped that within five years of INERELA+'s launch, the networks will increase their worldwide membership by over 6,000. These new members will mobilise their respective faith communities to provide accurate information and other services to an estimated 2.5 million people around the world, helping to reduce HIV-related silence, shame, stigma and discrimination, and thereby reducing the number of new infections.

Source: www.inerela.org

How can I help someone who has just found out they have HIV?

The person will probably be in some kind of shock as they come to terms with the situation. They may be afraid that you and others will reject them or their children.

The person may cope by not wanting to talk or even think about HIV or how they feel. They may carry on as if nothing has happened. Alternatively they may want to talk about it all the time, or may get depressed and become quiet and withdrawn. They may fear passing on HIV by mistake. They may feel guilty about how they got HIV, and about others they may have passed the virus on to. They may be angry at how they got HIV themselves. All of these things are normal, and the same person may flip from one state to another within a single day or even hour.

Listen; be slow to speak; very slow to offer advice. Try to discourage the person from making instant decisions that they may later regret. Remember that loneliness and fear of the future can be the hardest things to bear. Do not say, 'I know how you feel.' You will never know, but you can try to understand. Be ready with practical help, but do not rush in and take over someone's life. Do not talk to other people about their situation unless you have their permission to do so.

We are engaged to be married and one of us has tested positive for HIV. People are saying we should not marry. What should we do?

This is a common and very upsetting situation. An engaged couple where one has HIV and the other does not are entering a life-long relationship where the act of greatest intimacy could possibly kill one of them. For this reason, many church leaders in some parts of the world say that they will not marry couples unless they have been tested, and either both have HIV or both do not. However, while testing is a good idea, refusing to marry people is not helpful, in my view.

For a start, as we will see later, the actual risk of one passing on the virus to the other is very small if the person who has it is otherwise in good health, and if they use condoms carefully every time they have sex. Indeed it could be as low as 1 in 4,000 each time they make love,[4] or even less if the person with HIV is taking antiviral therapy regularly.

---

[4] Risk in normal intercourse can be around 1 in 200, but careful use of a condom can reduce that by up to 95 per cent, or 20 times less, and 20 times 200 is 4,000.

Engagement and marriage in West/Central Africa

'An engaged couple were told by their pastor to get tested just a week before their wedding. The groom turned out to be infected. Both families were really shocked. His parents were full of grief, as if he had already died. The wedding was cancelled. Fortunately, because the couple had not entered a sexual relationship, she was negative. We always tell pastors to encourage couples to be tested before the start of a serious relationship. At the same time we encourage testing for hepatitis and sickle cell.'

'A close member of my family was engaged to a young man. There were many disagreements about certain issues before his family would give their approval. After two years these issues were resolved and a wedding was planned. Five months before the wedding one of the couple tested positive for HIV. This is a major crisis for his family – especially as a dowry has already been paid for her. When the bride's family finds out, there will be huge pressure on them not to marry.'

'A trainee on one of our AIDS programmes was a woman who remained a virgin before marriage and was faithful afterwards. She gave birth to a baby that grew sick and died, and doctors discovered it was because of HIV infection. Her husband then died, but she has remained well on antivirals. In her widowhood she blamed God. Why did he allow her to be infected when she had been abstinent and faithful? Her pastor comforted her and later said he wanted to marry her. She said: "I have HIV." The pastor said: "It does not matter to me. God has clearly told me to marry you." They have now been happily married for five years. They do not have a child. She is head of women's ministries in the church. Most women in the church are confused because she has stayed so well. The husband is still negative. They are now preparing to try and get pregnant. They have been using condoms and her treatment has also made the risk of his infection very small.'

And even if the other of you were to test positive for HIV after some years (hopefully not likely), if you both receive antiviral therapy, it is possible that both of you could go on living reasonably normal lives for many more years.

All I am saying is that these are very complex and serious questions that need to be talked through very carefully, after prayer and reflection. All too often a couple decide to have a test very late – even the week before the wedding – so there is no time to think through what to do following a positive result.

People's lives have often been cruelly torn apart at such times by parents and other relatives. Marriages can suddenly be cancelled, and then many guests may find out about the test result before the person is ready for them to know.

For all these reasons it is really important for couples to get tested as early as possible in a relationship if there is any risk that either may have HIV. Couples should receive counselling before they are tested so that they have a chance to think through what they will do before they are given a test result. Church leaders can play a huge role here in educating church members, supporting engaged couples and supporting those who have HIV, as well as those who love them.

What about couples wanting to conceive a baby if one or both of them have HIV?

We should encourage people in such situations to be very caring and responsible, and to think very carefully before attempting to have children, because of the risk of infecting them, or leaving them as orphans at a young age. However, these are not decisions that the church should make for individuals; the church should simply provide good advice and support.

If a woman with HIV who is in reasonable health decides to have a baby, and she takes antivirals for at least 14 days before delivery, the risk of the baby being born with HIV is going to be less than 1 in 20. Without treatment, the risk could be around 1 in 3. Even a single dose of antivirals given to a mother in labour, and another dose given to the baby at birth, reduces the risk considerably.

Study results may vary, but the message is clear: the great majority of babies born to HIV-positive mothers will be healthy and live normal lives. With the best treatment, the risk of a mother with HIV giving birth to a child with HIV is very low.

Some still say the risk is too high for such a couple to attempt to have children. But we must be consistent. Imagine a woman in the church has been treated for breast cancer and doctors are hopeful she will live for at least 10 years more. Maybe she has been told she has a gene that could be passed on to her daughters, which could mean they get the same cancer when they are adults. Would you say that such a woman should not marry, or have a family? With good treatment, HIV infection can be a chronic condition, with people living 20 years or more. Most of their children will be healthy, and even if they are born with HIV, they may live well into adult life.

What about rumours of new 'cures'?

A lot of what you read and hear about cures for HIV infection or AIDS is rubbish. If it was that easy to find a cure, or if a vaccine really worked, doctors, nurses, hospitals and governments could stop worrying.

People with HIV die of various infections and problems that develop when HIV has weakened the body. So anything that helps the body get rid of these other infections can help someone make a dramatic recovery. They may go home from a hospital looking well, and are sometimes still completely well some months later. Until they get another infection, people may think they have been cured. This gives rise to rumours and many false reports. Although the person may be looking well, the situation may still be very serious. The same confusion can happen over claims of supernatural healing (see page 117).

How infectious is HIV?

Healthy skin is a good barrier against HIV. During normal sexual intercourse between a man and a woman, the risk is around 1 in 200 of infection from a single unprotected episode with a partner who has HIV, is well and without symptoms. But if one or other has an untreated sexually transmitted disease such as chancroid or gonorrhoea (causing sores and skin damage), then the risk of transmission could be 10 or 20 times higher. This is also true if the person is ill with AIDS.

The risk of infection is much higher if blood is injected into the body through using injecting equipment which has not been properly sterilised. It is also higher during rape, when delicate skin is damaged.

'I am confused because many people say certain things can give you HIV and other people say they cannot.'

Can you get HIV from a communion cup, or from sharing a glass? Or what about kissing, or swimming, or mosquitoes, or a toilet seat, or anything else like that? The answer is no. Nor can you get HIV from touching or hugging someone with HIV.

'You say that the virus cannot cross the skin unless there is a wound. But if that is true, how does it pass from a woman to a man, or the other way round?'

Skin on the penis of a man, and inside a woman, is sensitive, thin and delicate. Many totally painless, harmless, minute cracks appear in the skin of both partners when they make love. These are how the virus enters. As we have seen, any other sexually transmitted diseases will make the skin much more likely to bleed.

'How does HIV spread sexually from a man to a man?'

People often find it hard to talk about anal sex, but it is taking place more often than many people think, even in countries where such a practice is illegal. We are not just talking about men who have sex with men. Some heterosexual couples practise anal sex for a number of reasons (such as avoiding pregnancy), including the false belief that it will protect them against HIV transmission. Many men who have sex with men also have sex with women, so patterns of HIV spread are often complex.

If a man inserts his penis into the anus of a man or woman (this is known as anal sex), there is a significant risk of HIV being transmitted. Many people have become HIV-positive in this way. The risk is greater for the receiver, as there are cells inside the rectum which can be infected with HIV. Failure to use lubrication can mean small cracks in the skin are more likely, which can also increase the risk.

Some Christians react violently to this issue, and refuse to even think about offering any kind of help to men who have sex with men, to sex workers or to injecting drug users – but they should be very careful. God's love is to all people (John 3:16). All of us have fallen short of the glory of God (Romans 3:23). The more judgmental and intolerant a society is, the more certain people will hide away completely. The problem of HIV then gets forced underground. People are ashamed to be tested and reluctant to get treated. They meet in secret groups that no one can reach with health messages. HIV can then spread faster. (For more on issues of stigma and sexuality see Chapter 7.)

'Does male circumcision protect against HIV?'

Research in South Africa, Uganda and Kenya in 2007 strongly suggested that male circumcision reduces the risk of men becoming infected with HIV by around 60 per cent.

Up to 6 million new HIV infections and 3 million deaths could be prevented over the next 20 years if all men in sub-Saharan Africa were circumcised.

There are several possible reasons why circumcision has this effect. The foreskin creates a moist environment in which HIV can survive for longer. Also, if the foreskin is removed, then the skin on the head of the penis tends to become tougher and more resistant to infection.

However, circumcision is much less effective than condom use at preventing HIV transmission. If used consistently over the long term, condoms are at least 80 per cent effective, whereas circumcision only prevents around 60 per cent of infections. Safe circumcision requires trained staff, a clean clinic and sterile tools. Costs vary between $25 and $500 per person in Africa.

If people become too confident about protection from the effects of circumcision, they may engage in more high-risk sexual behaviour. Women may find it harder to insist on condom use by circumcised partners.

Many cultures have no tradition of circumcision, and some (including Hindus and Sikhs) are strongly opposed to it.

In addition, many agencies are working hard to eliminate female genital mutilation (FGM), a custom that is still common in some parts of the developing world. Promoting male circumcision may make it harder to stop FGM.[5]

'What are ABC, SAVE, SLOW and STOP prevention methods?'

ABC is the approach adopted for HIV prevention by the Uganda government and has been popular with many churches around the world. It stands for **A**bstinence, **B**e faithful, Use a **C**ondom. It has been effective because it is simple and easy to communicate.

---

[5] Text in this answer from AVERT

SAVE has been promoted by Christian Aid. It stands for **S**afer practices, **A**vailable medications, **V**oluntary testing and counselling, **E**mpowerment through education.

Rick Warren, leader of Saddleback Church, USA, and his wife Kay have been key in mobilising churches in America over HIV issues. He has proposed two approaches: **SLOW** and **STOP**. He suggests that churches will want to adopt **STOP** and wider society **SLOW**.

SLOW stands for **S**upply condoms, **L**imit numbers of partners, **O**ffer needle exchange, **W**ait for first onset of sex.

STOP stands for **S**ave sex for marriage, **T**each men to respect women and children, **O**ffer treatment through churches, **P**ledge yourself to one partner for life.

These can all be useful reminders of some ways to tackle HIV issues. There are many versions, but the truth is, as we have seen in this book, it is impossible to combine *all* important responses to HIV in all situations into a single short word.

'What is the connection between tuberculosis (TB) and HIV?'

TB is a bacterial infection spread through the air when an infectious person coughs, sneezes or even sings, just like the common cold. Most people who are infected with TB never go on to develop the disease. In most people who are infected with TB, the bacteria go to sleep deep down inside the lungs. This is called latent TB infection. It causes no symptoms and is not infectious. One third of the world's population has latent TB infection.

In some people, latent TB infection progresses to TB disease, usually because of poor nutrition, HIV or some other condition that weakens the body's defences. TB is the most common cause of illness and death among people living with HIV in many parts of the world. TB disease commonly causes symptoms such as a persistent cough lasting for more than two to three weeks, weight loss, fever, night sweats and coughing up blood.

It usually affects the lungs, but can also affect almost any part of the body. Without proper treatment TB will cause death in people living with HIV within weeks. However, TB is treatable, even in people living with HIV, especially if the diagnosis is made quickly before the person becomes too sick. TB disease is treated with a course of four antibiotics taken over at least six months. Any person living with HIV who has a cough lasting more than two weeks should go to their local health clinic and request a test for TB.[6]

What precautions need to be taken in hospitals and clinics?

Needles and syringes should not be used on more than one person without being properly sterilised. Fortunately almost every nation today has facilities to test all blood, as HIV can be transmitted through blood transfusions. But needles can also be in short supply, or equipment to heat and sterilise can be broken or unavailable.

Doctors and nurses have got HIV from those they care for during their medical work without knowing it, especially where hospitals have run out of gloves or following accidents. Health staff and volunteers need to be trained in safe medical practices. Health systems need to be resourced with equipment and supplies to protect their staff. Risk of infection can be reduced if a short course of antiviral treatment is given following accidental exposure. However, even without treatment, the risk of getting HIV following an injury from, say, a needle after taking blood from a patient is only around 1 in 200.

What about criminal aspects of HIV infection?

For most people living with HIV, preventing others from becoming infected with the virus they carry is a primary concern. HIV-positive individuals are, after all, only too aware of just how difficult it can be to live with the illness, and few would wish it on anybody else.

However, not all HIV-positive people take the precautions that they perhaps should. Is it morally right to prosecute someone for carelessly or purposely infecting another with an ultimately fatal virus? The assumption that it is, and its consequences, can present numerous problems. What are the issues that must be addressed when prosecuting someone for transmitting HIV? Is it right to try and criminalise HIV-positive people in this way?

First we need to understand the different types of transmission that can take place.

---

[6] Text of this answer written by Alasdair Reid, UNAIDS

What are the arguments for and against introducing legislation to make deliberate HIV infection a criminal act?

FOR	AGAINST
If you are HIV+, failing to use protection is wrong.	Criminalising HIV+ people increases stigma, particularly if the press demonises HIV-positive people.
Giving someone HIV is akin to murder.	HIV is an unpleasant virus to live with, but it is no longer a death sentence.
If you are HIV+, it is your duty to use protection.	The more cases that come to court, the more people will believe that the responsibility for having safe sex should lie solely with positive people.
Criminalising people for reckless transmission will act as a deterrent.	The law has no place in the bedroom, and has little effect on people's sexual behaviour.
It should be possible to call an HIV+ person 'reckless', even if they have never actually had an HIV test, since they have put themselves at risk in the past.	Prosecuting positive people could leave many afraid to be tested, believing that if they do find out their status, they could be liable to all sorts of criminal charges.
Putting people in prison will stop them from spreading HIV and endangering the community.	Imprisonment does nothing to help people come to terms with their HIV and take a safer attitude towards sex.
Criminal cases help lots of HIV+ people who might not otherwise learn their status.	Criminal cases give police licence to investigate the background of anyone they suspect of having passed on HIV.
Many laws relating to HIV could potentially be used to prevent people spreading many other fatal illnesses.	No other illnesses are treated with the same hysteria as HIV, and few people are ever criminalised for transmitting them.

Source: Adapted from AVERT

Deliberate: Most countries would consider this to be the most serious offence that can be committed. Transmission may be through needles or sex, with the primary purpose of transmitting the virus to another person.

Reckless: This is where HIV is passed on through a careless rather than deliberate act. If for example a person who knows they have HIV has unprotected sex with a negative person, but fails to inform them of the risk involved, this could be classed as reckless transmission in court.

Accidental: This is the most common way for HIV to be passed on. A person is generally said to have accidentally transmitted HIV if they were either unaware that they had the virus or if they were aware of their HIV-positive status and used a condom during sex, but the condom failed in some way.

Obtaining proof of the type of transmission can be exceedingly difficult and is normally done by comparing the DNA of the virus that each person is infected with. The very nature of sexual HIV transmission means there are no witnesses: what happens in the bedroom is essentially private.[7]

I have heard some people say that HIV does not cause AIDS

In a world of almost 6 billion people you will always find a small number with very strange ideas on any issue, and HIV is no different. Some people think global warming is not happening, that smoking does not cause cancer and so on. Despite overwhelming scientific research over 20 years, a few doctors, scientists and journalists still claim that there's no proof HIV causes AIDS. This is a very dangerous view, and is contrary to the huge amount of scientific evidence now available.

HIV has been isolated in all people with AIDS where such checks have been made. HIV attacks the same types of white cells that get damaged in people with AIDS. We know that antivirals that target the way HIV works inside human cells also help people with HIV live longer. We know that when HIV develops resistance to antivirals, the person becomes ill more quickly.

---

[7] Text of this answer adapted from AVERT

We know that babies born to mothers with HIV, who are infected themselves, die of AIDS-related diseases. Babies born without HIV do not develop AIDS.

People receiving blood transfusions containing HIV go on to develop AIDS. People who do not receive infected blood transfusions do not develop AIDS, unless infected with HIV in some other way.

Partners of people who test positive for HIV who later test positive themselves, go on to develop AIDS unless they receive proper treatment. Partners who remain uninfected do not. Drug users who use injecting equipment that is carrying HIV, and become infected, develop AIDS. Drug users who are using non-sterile injecting equipment that is carrying many other infections, but not HIV, do not become infected with HIV, and do not develop AIDS. When HIV infection levels rise in a local community, deaths from HIV-related conditions such as TB increase a few years later.

I find it strange that any intelligent, rational human being still has serious doubts that HIV causes AIDS. Ignoring research findings and health messages will put many people's lives at risk.

So then, we have looked at prevention and the questions people ask. Now we need to turn to urgent issues relating to women, orphans and vulnerable children, displaced peoples (refugees) and programmes for HIV counselling and testing.

CHAPTER FIVE

WOMEN, CHILDREN AND PEOPLE ON THE MOVE

HIV has had a huge impact on women, orphans, vulnerable children and refugees. What are the key issues? How should churches respond?

Women and HIV – a special challenge to the church

HIV has a female face in Africa, where 6 out of 10 new infections are among women. Women are not only more at risk in the sexual act with a partner who has HIV, but they also have fewer opportunities to avoid infection. They may be physically abused, targets of terrible war-related sexual violence, abandoned to raise children or ignored by authorities.

Inequality between men and women fuels the spread of HIV. For example, women receive only 10 per cent of the world's income, 66 per cent of those in the world who cannot read are women and 99 per cent of property owners are men. Gender-based violence causes more deaths and disability among women aged 15 to 44 than cancer, malaria, traffic accidents and war. And 85 per cent of those displaced by wars and disasters are women and children.

Preventing HIV – infection in girls and young women – UNAIDS

Some 7,000 girls and women become infected with HIV every day. In most regions, women and girls make up an increasing proportion of the population living with HIV, and rates of female infection continue to rise – particularly in Eastern Europe, Asia and Latin America. In South Africa, Zambia and Zimbabwe, women aged 15 to 24 are five to six times more likely to be infected than young men of the same age.

Challenging men's attitudes to women in Africa

Improving relationships between men and women is one of the most powerful and effective ways to prevent HIV transmission. Tearfund UK has been working in partnership with two local organisations, one in Burkina Faso and the other in Zimbabwe, to change attitudes of men and women towards each other and to themselves.

Through Enjoy Your Marriage courses, youth camps and taking a holistic approach to gender and HIV education and awareness, the project has seen dramatic and life-changing results.

Pauline and Amos live in a village in Natisa, rural Zimbabwe. They were married in June 2008 after living together for over eight years. The decision to marry came after they attended the Church Family Relationships programme run by CAT.

Pauline says, 'Before, we used to argue a lot and go off in different directions. Now that has changed. We listen to each other and speak softly to each other.' Amos agrees, 'Yes, before I was a drunkard. I used to be irresponsible and blow money. Now the atmosphere is changed. It is nice and enjoyable. We communicate better.'

Things have improved too in their intimate relationship. 'Before, sex was just turn around and get on with it. It was hurried. I used to tell him to hurry up because I wanted to get on with my jobs. Sex was a real struggle for me. Now we talk and agree when we are having sex. We use different techniques. It is much better now. I enjoy it thoroughly. I look forward to him coming back from the fields,' enthuses Pauline.

Amos adds, 'The programme taught me that men and women are equal. I changed. I now help my wife in the home, such as cutting up vegetables. My friends and neighbours say I've been given a love potion by my wife, but I don't care. I love my wife and I tell everyone that I love my wife.'

In bringing a holistic approach, including challenging culture that restricts, restrains and subjugates men and women, the project has seen life-changing results. It has brought life and light in the midst of the HIV pandemic.

A Tearfund pilot initiative with Vigilance, Burkina Faso, and Christian AIDS Taskforce [CAT] in Zimbabwe – interviews by Mandy Marshall

Women who are married can be in particular danger from partners with HIV, and it can be almost impossible for them to avoid this – either by refusing their husband's sexual advances if they suspect he has been unfaithful, or by insisting they use condoms.

A West African pastor said to me recently that in his culture, if a man finds his wife has tested positive for HIV, he often abandons her. If a woman finds her husband has HIV, she may just say something like: 'I have always followed him, and I will follow him to the grave.'

In churches we often have a romantic view of family life. Family is central to God's purpose for human beings. We hope and pray that in the majority of cases, church families are happy places where there is faithfulness in married couples, and where children are loved and protected.

Yet all pastors know that the family can sometimes be a dangerous place for women and children. Women may be beaten up by drunken husbands, and young girls and boys abused sexually, by fathers, stepfathers or other male family members. We must not keep silent about these terrible things, which can be much more common than we realise.

We can start in our churches by encouraging men to respect women. Some traditional HIV-prevention strategies have tended to focus on **ABC** (**A**bstain, **B**e faithful, Use a **C**ondom). While this has undoubtedly prevented large numbers of people from becoming infected, many of the world's women are not in a position to abstain from sex, rely on fidelity or negotiate condom use.

Many steps can be taken to help empower women, and to encourage self-confidence and culturally appropriate ways to try to protect themselves. However, it is clear that it is also really important to change the attitudes and behaviour of men. That is why teams like ACET Uganda have special projects to target men.

The Bible teaches us that men and women are equal in the sight of God, both made in his image (Genesis 1:27). Churches and Christian organisations can start by acknowledging the problem and talking about it. We should include women in this conversation and listen to their stories about the hidden realities of their daily lives. We should talk about the example of Jesus, and the way he shocked the leaders of the time by going out of his way to welcome, befriend and protect women – even those whose lifestyles were considered shameful.

Many church leaders point out Bible verses that talk about the man as the head of the household. But the apostle Paul also teaches husbands to love their wives as Jesus loves the church: with deep compassion, respect and care (Ephesians 5:25–28).

Christians should study biblical teaching, sensitively challenge unhelpful practices and customs, and do all that is possible to support and protect the marginalised and oppressed, and to work with women to empower choices. However, we also need to respect cultures and traditions. There is always a risk that a big promotion of women's rights by those in wealthy nations may be seen as yet another form of

Improve sexual and reproductive health services for all – UNAIDS

Worldwide, only 1 in 5 people who need reproductive health services actually have access to them. There may not be any facilities near enough. Even if people can get to facilities, they may not be able to pay the fees charged.

Girls and women may be reluctant to seek advice for fear of stigmatisation. They may be put off by unhelpful and discriminatory staff.

HIV-prevention strategies must meet the needs of women living with HIV. Positive women need to be able to access sexual and reproductive health services without fear of stigma and discrimination. When people living with HIV can feel comfortable with being open about their status, and where they can receive counselling and treatment to keep them healthy for longer and have a safe and satisfying sex life, they are far less likely to pass the virus on to others.

aggressive cultural imperialism – a 'we know best' attitude. There are many, many things in the culture of wealthy nations that should be a cause of shame rather than pride, including an obsession with materialism and destroying the planet's resources. So let us all proceed with humility, willing to listen and understand.

Orphans and vulnerable children (OVCs)

When we are talking about support of women, we also need to think about their children. Many AIDS-related deaths are of young parents who leave orphaned children. There are already 11 million AIDS orphans, and many millions more who are vulnerable because of HIV. For example, a young child may be looking after two sick parents at home, as well as younger brothers and sisters.

The ideal place for almost all orphans is within a loving family, together with their brothers and sisters, in a household with similar culture, language and values, in the community where they were born. However, this is not always possible. Sometimes options to keep children in their community break down. Workers may be forced to choose between alternatives, each of which may involve risks and is less than ideal.

The track record of orphanages has not always been good, with problems of child sex abuse, neglect, cruelty and emotional deprivation. That is why so many international donors are cautious about orphanages today.

However, smaller informal kinds of institution, with small numbers of children in each 'family' unit, may be a better option. Take time to listen to those who are in each community, and then listen some more. Visit the places where such children are living, and other places where they could be – or listen to others who have visited such places recently.

ACET teams have recently had to become involved in supporting institutions for children in many different countries. Even though their desire is always for a child to live in the community, they have found many situations where it cannot happen. They have needed (reluctantly perhaps) to commit resources to improve orphan care centres in some way, even if just in supporting and training staff. Such countries include Thailand, Russia, Uganda, Zimbabwe, South Africa, India, Belarus, Czech Republic and Central Asian republics.

In some countries the extended family usually takes care of orphaned children. But in many villages and towns there are so many children to take care of that extended families cannot cope. Sometimes those children end up being used as servants and may be sexually abused. Churches need to make sure that all children are well treated and loved.

Situations where alternative care may be needed

Here are some situations where alternatives may be needed for children:

- Refugee and displaced people's camps, or war zones where large numbers of children are orphans or vulnerable, and normal community support has broken down.
- Child-headed households where it becomes impossible to continue supporting children in their own homes. Maybe the oldest 12-year-old child is now sick, or the neighbours cannot provide enough help.
- Babies or children abandoned/rejected in larger numbers than can be placed in local communities.
- Local villages or towns overwhelmed with the death of parents and other carers.
- Children in cities where there is a breakdown of community ties and they are at risk of ending up on the streets unsupervised, out of school, seduced, kidnapped, raped or worse.

HIV orphans: Choose to Care, Southern Africa

Successful models for orphan care:

- Day care shelters that provide food, medical care and education to orphans who otherwise are looked after by grandparents or elder relatives.

- Although the ideal is to keep children in their communities, it is not always possible. In some cases, they are ostracised by neighbours and even by relatives and cannot count on anyone to look after them in their local communities. Thus institutional care, while not ideal, becomes a necessity.

- In many places programmes sponsor feeding schemes where orphans can access at least one nutritious meal per day after school.

- Where children prefer to stay with older brothers and sisters, church-related programmes assist such child-headed households. Thembalethu has a network of more than a hundred monitors and care-givers who visit children daily and ensure provision for their health, nutrition and clothing needs.

- In rural areas, where traditional family structures remain strong, orphans are placed in traditional homesteads. These homesteads are strengthened financially (mainly through agricultural development) to care for the increased number of children.

- In urban areas, focus is often on recreating a family setting. Six or seven orphans are placed in a house with an adult 'mother' or 'father' to look after them.

- The ultimate goal of some programmes is placement of these children in adoption or long-term foster care.

- Orphans are also assisted with scholarships and other means to enable them to stay in school.

A faith-based response to HIV in Southern Africa: the Choose to Care initiative, UNAIDS best practice collection

- Children who have already lived for some years in an orphanage that is functioning reasonably well but has real and urgent practical needs – for example, leaking roofs, no mosquito nets for beds, no clean drinking water, no proper sewerage, poor diet, no money for education or basic medicines.

Every child is different and unique in God's eyes. They will differ in age, culture, personality, emotional stability, recent history, whether they have brothers and sisters who should be kept together and so on. Decisions must be made about each child, taking into account all local factors. Older children's views are also very important. Parents who are dying may also make strong requests about the future care of their own children, which should always be followed wherever possible.

Adoption of AIDS orphans?

International adoption should always be a last resort. It is vital that every other opportunity should be explored first within the child's own community.

International adoption is a risky route both for the child and for their receiving family. Culture shock, language change, identity crisis, climate adjustments and emotional trauma can often result if adoption happens after the first or second birthday. Brothers and sisters can also end up separated, because it is rare that a family will adopt several orphans at the same time.

However, there is growing infertility in many wealthy nations and a huge shortage of babies for adoption because so many unwanted pregnancies end in abortion. As a result, there are very large numbers of people anxious to adopt, and a growing number are willing to adopt HIV orphans.

It is not practical and often not appropriate to restrict help only to those orphaned by HIV. For a start, when you enter a village and a hundred orphans gather round, how can you be certain why each child lost their parents? Most may indeed be HIV orphans, but do consider including those orphaned from other causes (or indeed all the children), or you may cause bitter resentment.

House of Grace, Thailand

In southern Thailand, Pastor Kitisak and his wife were praying about the HIV situation. Pastor Kitisak was leading a small church, when

50,000 orphans – HOPE HIV – Phil and Wendy Wall

Hope HIV is supporting around 50,000 children and young people through some 40 partner organisations in 400 communities in sub-Saharan Africa. It started after Phil and Wendy Wall visited South Africa from the UK.

'We were deeply moved during a visit to Africa in 1997, and tried to adopt a young orphaned girl called Zodwa, who had touched our hearts. Her parents had died of AIDS-related disease. We were blocked by legal issues for over six months. During this waiting period we began to think some more about the whole process and possible alternative ways to help other children in the same situation. Then her own grandmother was found, who was delighted to look after her. Out of this experience, we started to do what we could to raise money to fund support for local communities for thousands of HIV orphans across Africa.

One of those young people is Jeffrey, who lives at the Palabek Gem displaced people's camp in northern Uganda. He was 14 when he joined the Orphan Affairs Council, an initiative supported by HOPE HIV, which oversees the rights, needs and voices of 500 orphaned and vulnerable children in the camp. Jeffrey has been appointed Minister for Resource Mobilisation, and makes sure that food and donated clothes reach those most in need. With HOPE HIV funds, Jeffrey has now completed a one-year course in construction, and will take an active role in rebuilding his country's future.'

www.hopehiv.org

people started bringing to his home children who had been totally rejected by local people after their parents had died from AIDS. The Kitisaks began to add these children to their own family, and cared for them all in their own home. And more kept arriving. Some of these children also had the HIV infection themselves.

Before long Pastor Kitisak managed to rent a small empty school building, into which they all moved together. This was their home for several years, but it was run down and the roof leaked, so Pastor Kitisak began to pray for a new home.

Working with Alan and Maelynn Ellard, who had led ACET Thailand for 16 years, they raised funding to build a completely new facility, with different houses that could each accommodate around 12 children, with a treatment wing for the sick. ACET Thailand had a long track record of community care for people with HIV in Bangkok and further north, as well as church mobilisation and support groups for women with HIV.

They all moved into the House of Grace in December 2007. It has been a long journey, but the children have a settled, beautiful and peaceful home at last.

The relationship with Pastor Kitisak's church has not always been easy. He no longer leads it, but remains actively involved, as well as running the House of Grace and ACET Thailand. Some in the church find it hard to cope with 60 lively AIDS orphans who are, of course, a dominant group on Sunday mornings.

Issues to consider about orphans

Here are some big issues to think about. Should we care only for AIDS orphans, or should that care extend to those orphaned for other reasons – and how can we tell? What do we mean by 'orphan' – a child who has lost both parents or only one?

Be aware that it is always easier to touch people's hearts and raise funds with orphan stories than it is to raise funds for prevention work, but the challenge must be to prevent a future generation of orphans. So make sure you build prevention into every orphan programme.

Psychosocial support for orphans and vulnerable children is really important. Such work has been pioneered by organisations such as REPSSI, which is now active in 13 African nations. World Vision, the Nehemiah Project, UNICEF and others now give greater attention to the emotional well-being and social support of children impacted by HIV.

Summary on responding to orphans

- Raise orphans' living situation to the same level as their peers, but no higher, to prevent resentment.
- Enable orphans, if possible, to live in their own home and community, with access to land.
- Place orphans in extended families if you can.
- Encourage non-institutional options if possible.
- Agree at what age support will end.
- Remember that orphan support is a very long-term commitment to particular children.
- Think about microfinance options or business training for when schooling ends.
- Involve older orphans and listen to them.
- Empower families and communities by training and supporting them.

Matilda Trust – the story of Richard and Wendy Phillips

'We were working in Zimbabwe in 1998. Passing through the communal lands, we saw homestead after homestead with recent marked graves in the compound. We got a sense of the frightening enormity of the HIV crisis. We would wonder what it was like to be trying to care for your partner or son or daughter with so few resources available. Or how it is to be the parent of young children, knowing you are dying and leaving them utterly vulnerable. And the need in us to bring some relief grew.

One particular young woman with HIV, Matilda Ncube, touched our hearts. She became a friend and died in 1999, leaving her 15-year-old son. From that point AIDS became personal. Not a vast pandemic that touches many others, but a disease that killed our beloved friend. Matilda already had AIDS when we first met her, and she lived with the knowledge that she would die of it before long. Like the many other trials in her life, she accepted this with a quiet dignity.

If AIDS is too big for a few people to change, at least we could try to help those dying to end their lives in a little more comfort. The area where there was the greatest need was for packs for home-based care volunteers. They often work without soap, gloves, etc.

Today, Matilda Trust is providing support from Ireland and other nations to over 3,000 orphans in Zimbabwe, as well as 4,000 adults ill with AIDS at home. This has not been an easy task – inflation briefly ran at around 1 billion per cent a year. Community teams use a model similar to that developed by Scripture Union and REPSSI. Trained volunteers go into homes, looking out for child-headed households. Each household looking after orphans receives regular food packs, and school fees for orphans are sometimes paid. Many orphans are fed each day as part of a school programme.'

- Provide wider support than just for those whose parents have died of AIDS-related diseases.
- Be aware and prepared for some orphans to have HIV and to need medical care.
- Provide skills that will sustain families, such as farming and other income-generation activities.
- Be prepared to provide institutional care if some orphans cannot be placed in the community for various reasons.
- If institutional care is needed, try hard to keep each unit small and to create a sense of family.
- Give regular food parcels to individuals or families.
- Provide school fees and clothes.
- Provide school breakfasts – some children in very deprived areas

may walk up to three hours to and from school each day, not having eaten at home before they leave.

- Provide visits and support from a key worker, plus a link to a family or volunteer.
- Provide special training for the oldest child in child-headed households.

Other useful resources: www.jlica.org

Counselling and testing for HIV – for prevention and care

Counselling and testing programmes are very important ways to identify those who need treatment for HIV, as well as their unborn children, who can be protected with antivirals. Such programmes also help with behaviour change across the community.

ACET in the Democratic Republic of Congo runs such a counselling and testing programme. Teams go into schools, churches, youth groups, colleges and other community settings. They know that 6 per cent of adults across the nation have HIV, but there has been little HIV prevention and many churches are only now waking up to the situation. When they talk to groups about HIV, many people are shocked and start worrying about their HIV status. They ask how they can get tested.

There are only a few government centres in Kinshasa, serving 8 million people, so the team began testing people themselves. First, each person receives counselling. Why do they want a test? Have they really been at risk? Do they understand what the test will tell them? How will they react if the test is positive or negative? What action will they want to take if the result is negative or positive? Who will they tell? And so on.

They are then offered a test. This is carried out by a trained laboratory worker using an instant testing kit. Three different tests are carried out. If the first test is positive, the second is carried out. If the second test is also positive it is confirmed with a third test. If all three are positive, it is almost certain the person has HIV (less than one mistake in 300). The tests cost around $3 each, and can be done while the person waits.

If the test is positive, the person receives special support as they begin to work through what it means for them. Every person who is

HIV-positive is followed up and introduced to government medical teams, with the hope of getting access to free antivirals. If antivirals are not available, the team may try to fill the gap by starting the person on treatment until more government supplies start coming through.

If teenagers ask about testing they are told to discuss it with their parents, so testing becomes a family decision. In some nations, a teenager's conversation about HIV risks is considered totally private, and government clinics may offer a test without the consent of the parents.

Armed conflict often makes HIV spread faster. Most wars today are within nations rather than between them, causing millions of refugees to flee. When law and order breaks down and armed militia roam the streets, it is impossible to run a health service. Prevention campaigns collapse and disease spreads. Groups of armed men often take many sexual partners, either at gunpoint (using rape as a weapon of war) or in return for favours. This has been a huge problem in the Democratic Republic of Congo and other parts of Central Africa, with hundreds of thousands of girls and women caught up in conflicts.

Ways in which organisations can get involved in medical care programmes related to HIV testing and counselling activities

- Provide education about treatment availability.
- Identify pregnant mothers in rural areas who are missed by existing healthcare systems – 40 per cent of Indian women give birth at home.
- Teach pregnant mothers about the advantages of being tested.
- Provide access to pre- and post-test counselling.
- Carry out HIV tests and give confidential results.
- Make sure all pregnant women who test positive for HIV enrol in antiviral programmes.
- Provide training and support for people to help them take their medication correctly and at the right time(s).
- Monitor long-term treatment for serious side effects.
- Provide nutritional support to all those with HIV.
- Help prevent and treat other infections common in those with HIV. This is one of the most effective ways to help extend the life of the 80 per cent of people with HIV who have no access to antivirals.

The three Cs

UNAIDS only supports testing of individuals who have themselves chosen to be tested. All testing should be conducted under the conditions of the three Cs:

- Informed **Consent**
- Be **Confidential**
- Include **Counselling**.

Where there are high levels of stigma and discrimination and a low capacity to deliver testing and counselling under the three Cs, these issues should be addressed first.

There should be a realistic expectation of access to antivirals if tests are positive. There should also be access to prevention, care and support.

Source: UNAIDS/WHO guidelines

- Treat other sex diseases, such as gonorrhoea, that can accelerate spread and also cause people with HIV to become ill more quickly.

Refugees and displaced people

You can set up a wonderful HIV clinic, with testing and counselling, but in many parts of the world the situation may become unstable and such facilities may no longer be in the right place, or be out of action.

HIV spreads rapidly when communities break up or are on the move, or when ill-disciplined armies roam the countryside, and rape or child abductions are common. There are over 15 million refugees in the world, often living in terrible conditions, in crowded camps with poor sanitation, little healthcare and few schools. Some 75 per cent of these refugees are in nations where there is a high incidence of HIV.

In emergency situations, HIV often seems less important than food, shelter, water, emergency healthcare and security. But long-term issues need to be addressed at the same time.

Northern Uganda has been disrupted for over 20 years by a group called the Lord's Resistance Army, which terrorised the population, killing villagers, burning their homes, slaughtering cattle, destroying crops and taking children. These young people were often then drugged, beaten, armed and forced back to their home villages to kill members of their own families, with threats that they would be shot themselves if they refused. Thousands of these brutalised children, led by militia, were hiding in the bush.

As a result, tens of thousands of subsistence farmers ended up living in government compounds, where they were expected to build their own mud huts and somehow survive without being able to live anywhere near their own land. Up to 60,000 people were crammed into these camps, surrounded not by barbed-wire or fences, but by several hundred metres of grassland, where forest had been cleared so that militia could be seen before attacks.

The whole area has been very dangerous at times for project workers, with camps overrun by mobs, armed roadblocks and frequent ambushes in remote areas. ACET teams have maintained a continuous presence throughout the troubles. They have worked with traumatised youth, educated thousands about HIV and other sexually transmitted diseases, helped provide basic healthcare, and helped to strengthen the capacity of many other agencies.

General refugee lessons
- Huge risks from multiple sexual partners in camps.
- Breakdown of social traditions, discipline and culture.
- Needs can be very urgent, complex and rapidly changing.
- Church structures may take time to form.
- Work needs to be in partnership with community leaders.
- Situation needs to be viewed as a whole, to see how projects will fit into wider strategy.
- Partnership and communication with other agencies is really important.
- Communities reward project workers who have the courage not to run away with great respect and trust, which can open many doors to make things happen, both in the community as a whole and in changing individual behaviour.
- One day (hopefully) instability in the area will settle and camps will get smaller, as villagers return. Some camps may develop into permanent large villages or small towns, even when the situation is totally stable.

Poverty alleviation and income-generation activities

Women living with HIV, orphans, child-headed households, displaced peoples – they are all more likely than the general population to have one thing in common: daily challenges in finding enough income to buy food and survive.

There has been a huge amount of publicity about micro-banking and microfinance – and their power to generate wealth for millions of people. Income generation can indeed be a practical way to support families, but it must be set up with care and skill. People with HIV may have difficulties paying back loans if they become ill. It may be necessary to help at such times with small grants. An alternative is to include the wider family in the servicing of the loan and running the business.

Issues for income generation

- Previous experience in running such projects is essential.
- Skills required may be very specific – training may be needed.
- Churches or projects running such loan schemes must be sure it fits with their culture and values.
- Each business idea must be likely to be viable.
- There needs to be a market and the person must have the necessary skills.
- Expert help should be sought to test these issues.
- Loans in most schemes are for women – but this can lead to increased burdens rather than self-reliance.
- Lessons should be learned from other organisations doing similar work.

HIV advocacy – challenge our world

So what do you do when you are struggling to provide enough care and support for very vulnerable and marginalised people? What tools can you use to challenge government inaction or cultural taboos?

Every effective HIV programme is likely to become involved in advocacy: helping the voice of those with HIV to be heard; fighting stigma, injustice and prejudice. This might involve talking to doctors at a local hospital who keep turning people with HIV away. It may involve talking to local community leaders to make sure that HIV orphans are allowed to attend the school. Advocacy may involve giving interviews to newspapers or on radio and TV, campaigning for more pregnant women to be able to get access to free treatment and so on.

Advocacy really matters: speaking up for the victimised, oppressed, vulnerable and marginalised. We are called to be God's voice. We need to pray that we will win people, not antagonise them. We may need to be diplomatic and tactful rather than aggressive and demanding. My experience is that moral courage is always respected, even if people do not agree with you. It is important to recognise that the person you are talking to may have many other pressures and issues to deal with. Be understanding of their position.

You must be able to risk a relationship, or you will be muzzled and intimidated. However, do seek advice before taking a major and controversial public stand on an issue which could affect other Christian work. You could find that the media attention you raise on one issue results in the closure of many other projects – even people being thrown out of the country.

Issues for advocates

- Develop relationships with key people and organisations.
- Encourage those with HIV to speak for themselves.
- Try not to speak on behalf of those with HIV and their families unless they agree.
- Facilitate meetings between marginalised groups and people with power.
- Be aware that prejudices and fears are often strong and take time to change.
- Remember that advocacy happens at many levels, local and national.

We have looked at how HIV particularly affects women, the impact on orphans, vulnerable children and displaced people, and the role of advocacy. But now we need to turn to one of the most common ways that churches have been supporting people living with HIV: home support or community-based care.

CHAPTER SIX

HOW TO CARE FOR PEOPLE AT HOME

Twenty Nigerian pastors are sitting in a circle in a remote rural village. They have been sharing their responses at the end of the week-long training programme. 'So what is God calling you to do? What has he laid on your heart?'

The decisions they make in the next hour or two will result in tens of thousands of young people being reached with prevention messages, thousands of church members agreeing to be tested and many new support groups for those with HIV, as well as for orphans and widows.

You need neither funds nor a large team to start. It costs nothing to care for a friend or neighbour, or to talk to your own children, colleagues or church leaders about HIV, or to include HIV issues in your church teaching programme, or work training schemes, or school curriculum. Together we can make a huge difference.

You may not be able to help all those with HIV or orphaned by AIDS, but you can give practical help and encouragement to a few. If you live in an area where HIV is not yet a significant problem, you can support those working in harder-hit places through prayer and funding.

Here are nine different stories to encourage you. They are from Zimbabwe, Ireland, India, Zambia, the UK, Uganda and Nigeria. You may be able to adapt some of the ideas into your own situation.

Every one of these stories has a small beginning. An individual touched by the love of God. People who felt they *had* to do something, and who began, usually with almost nothing, step by step, following God's calling, in fellowship with others and learning from those around them as they went.

In many cases the road was long because there were few role

models for such programmes at the time. But now the programmes they began are an inspiration and practical encouragement to us.

These community care programmes are only half the story. As we have seen, care is not enough. We also need to stop more lives being lost at the same time, by preventing new infection and enabling more people with HIV to get earlier treatment.

These projects are examples of the many tens of thousands of Christian HIV initiatives run by believers, in local churches of all denominations, or with their close support.

Some people rush to raise money to build new hospitals or clinics or orphanages, but building projects usually take a long time, cost a lot, and the huge running costs may make them unsustainable. They are rarely what is needed first. On the other hand, groups of volunteers can start today, as part of a local church, doing what churches have always been good at.

What will really change the HIV situation is a people movement, not grand projects which only touch a small group of people. What is needed are millions more men and women stirred into action, carrying life-saving messages wherever they go, and showing practical, loving compassion as part of their daily lives.

Making HIV work a part of what we do

HIV affects all aspects of development, so we need to include it in what happens in all other programmes – in a way that clearly makes a difference. For example, traditional birth attendants can also help with HIV awareness and encourage pregnant women to be tested for HIV, so that they and their babies can be protected with antivirals.

People living with HIV need to be consulted. We should allow them to inform us of their needs. They can give critical insights into a programme's work and they should be fully integrated into the programme development.

Caring for all who need our help

Our care must be totally non-judgemental, compassionate and loving. It should be offered to all affected by HIV, regardless of how they came to be in need of help. Our care is unconditional because the love of Jesus is unconditional, offered to all. Our care is open to all – men and women, old and young, every tribal group or religious affiliation

– regardless of sexual orientation, regardless of sexual behaviour or other things, such as whether they have injected drugs.

All care of those with HIV-related illness needs to be 'holistic': different people have different needs that may be physical, emotional, social or spiritual. The balance of these needs can change from hour to hour and we need to be very sensitive to what the person wants or doesn't want from us today.

Examples of different types of care programme

Here are some different kinds of care programme:

- **Integration:** HIV care is part of general health services or general church activities. No new organisation is created. The advantage is that it is efficient and can reduce stigma. The disadvantage is that in many ways HIV is different from other viral infections or medical conditions and requires rapid responses. If everything is integrated, HIV work can be lost in all the other priorities – are we making a fruit salad or a mashed-up fruit juice which loses its character?
- **Specialist centres/HIV-specific clinics:** These may be needed in many areas, providing excellent services that can complement government services. They cost much less than specialist hospitals. Beware of creating a 'privileged group' if these specialist centres offer better care for HIV than is available elsewhere.
- **Volunteer/community-based model:** This uses friends, family, neighbours and church volunteers. It is often low cost and can grow quickly, providing home care, prevention and other support.
- **National mobilisation:** Churches can mobilise entire communities – for example, by training village care assistants who can reach large numbers of people quickly. They can assist with the diagnosis and treatment of common diseases, such as malaria and dysentery, as part of HIV programmes.
- **Centres of excellence:** Centres of excellence are important in all kinds of HIV work – showing what can be done, raising standards and providing places where people from other organisations can come and be trained. Centres of excellence provide technical advice, and can help organisations to grow faster in a more sustainable way. (See next chapters.)

1. Community care in rural African setting – FACT, Zimbabwe

First let us look at how community care developed in Zimbabwe. Dr Geoff Foster founded FACT (Family AIDS Caring Trust) in Mutare, in 1988. He was moved by children and parents whose lives were being destroyed by HIV, and his own hospital was in danger of being overwhelmed. After much prayer and discussion, he formed a home-care team to mobilise churches. They provided volunteers who were trained to give basic care at home, overseen by FACT healthcare workers and volunteer leaders.

Volunteers are trained in care and emotional support. They help with things like washing and personal hygiene, washing clothes and bed linen, house cleaning, provision of food and the dressing of small wounds. They started just looking after those with HIV, but later included people with TB, diabetes, malaria and other conditions.

The team supports family members who may be doing most of the caring. Volunteers offer advice about health issues common to those with HIV, as well as information on other community services.

This low-cost model has grown rapidly and been successful because local church leaders are totally committed to it. Volunteers keep careful notes about visits, which also helps the government and donors to understand the size of the problem, and what is being done about it.

Summary on community care

- Community-based care reaches more people and usually costs less than hospital care.
- People with HIV usually want to stay in their own homes.
- It might be necessary to care for those with other illnesses as well.
- Families, friends, communities and volunteers are key resources – but need training and support.
- Care needs to be holistic: physical, emotional, social and spiritual.
- Care teams work best when linked in partnership with other services, such as local hospitals.
- Volunteers can help with antiviral treatment, ensuring regular supplies and encouraging people to take medication regularly, as well as monitoring their general health.
- Careful selection, training and support of volunteers is vital.
- Each volunteer should be clear about what they are expected to do, and when they should ask staff for advice.

- A small amount of financial help might need to be offered to key volunteers.
- Volunteers should be monitored and supported, and brought together regularly for training and encouragement.
- Volunteers and other members of the community, including representatives of those you are helping, should be involved in decisions about the programme. The more it is 'owned' by them, the less you will have to do yourself, and the more sustainable the programme will be.
- Programmes owned by local communities often multiply as one community inspires another.

2. Community care for injecting drug users – ACET Ireland

Community care often takes a different form in developed nations like Ireland. Dublin has a serious HIV problem, often related to drug injecting. Terry Coleman-Black felt deeply touched by God about the people she met in this city. Many were in terrible situations, with lots of children living in households where drugs were being taken every day, where there was often a degree of chaos and where parents were becoming sick with AIDS. Many people were unsympathetic, including care workers and some from government agencies.

Terry began to go into homes in 1992, doing what she could, and soon had a small group of church volunteers doing the same. The work has grown, with several full-time staff, part-timers and volunteers supporting around 30 to 40 people and many children of those who have died. The service is 'client-focused', which means that those who are requesting help do so on their own terms, and what is provided is shaped by their own views.

The programme was set up as part of ACET in Ireland. They were one of the first agencies to work across the national border, encouraging peace, harmony and understanding, as well as mobilising churches to provide care and save lives.

Many people expected problems from religious leaders, especially about education messages, but ACET educators have been welcomed into both Catholic and Protestant schools.

More than 120 families have received support in Dublin – whether practical help, emotional support, bereavement support or family therapy. The Dublin team has also reached more than 150,000 in schools, colleges, churches and other places with prevention messages and training.

Dublin home care – lessons learned

- Bear in mind that special approaches are often needed when looking after drug users with HIV.
- Make sure the whole family is part of your care plan.
- Involve clients in every stage of planning.
- Expect that some people in the community may not approve of your work – even in the church.
- Remember that children may feel a huge burden of responsibility to watch over their sick and drug-dependent parents.
- Be flexible in your plans, as those you are supporting may find planning ahead very difficult.
- Be ready for long-term bereavement support of children left behind – your group may be the only place they feel able to talk about what has happened.

3. Clinic-based care – Nireekshana ACET, Hyderabad, India

India is very different from African nations, yet some issues are the same when it comes to community care for those living with HIV. In 2004 Dr Sujai Suneetha and his wife Lavanya received their first visitor with AIDS at their home, sent by a local pastor. They had both been involved in leprosy care for many years and had become deeply burdened by the terrible situations faced by the growing number of people with HIV in India. What was God calling them to do?

Gradually local pastors and other community health workers started to send more people. Sujai and Lavanya soon had to give up their work in leprosy care in order to help those who came. Around 60 new people came to their home each month, in addition to existing patients who were returning regularly. They and their family were soon under great pressure. With support from local Christians, they managed to move the clinic out of their home and into an office in a busy street.

Sujai's approach is simple: treat each person with a really warm welcome, with gentleness, deep respect and sensitivity. They may have experienced terrible rejection since diagnosis. He asks about their home and family situation and whether they are still able to work. He makes sure each person has the opportunity to talk with a counsellor, and to receive spiritual support, if that is what they would like.

Many patients are given simple, low-cost medicines such as anti-biotics, plus vitamins and nutritional supplements. People with HIV often become weak because they feel too unwell to eat properly, or have lost their jobs and cannot afford good food. Antibiotics help overcome existing infections and help prevent new infections when the immune system is damaged. If the person qualifies for free antivi-ral treatment in a government clinic, a staff member may accompany them. Sometimes it is hard work to overcome the reluctance of some doctors to give treatment and proper care, especially if the person is getting worse and needs hospital admission.

The clinic has a small but well-equipped laboratory that is able to test for HIV and a variety of other infections common in HIV. Many in the clinic are volunteers, including doctors and nurses, mostly from India. Data is kept on patient attendance patterns, problems, treatment given and survival. This is vital for planning, monitoring, evaluation and research.

The team provides very low-income families with modest financial support to keep their children in school, and has developed a church mobilisation and HIV-prevention programme. Once a week teams visit some of the urban slums to hold clinics in church halls for people too sick or poor to travel.

The Nireekshana model is relatively simple, requiring very little technology. It has been taught rapidly to doctors and other health-care workers and, less than five years from starting, Nireekshana has seeded more than six other clinics in neighbouring regions, with plans to add many more.

Clinic-based care – lessons learned

- Warmly welcome all who come – they may have experienced a lot of rejection since knowing they have HIV.
- Take time with each person who comes – it means a huge amount to those with HIV.
- Be sensitive to each person's situation, and what is happening in their whole family.
- Look for low-cost, simple treatment options that can make a big impact. Antibiotics such as Cotrim can be effective in preventing new infections.

- Use a large team so that each person will feel well cared for, even if they are only able to spend a short time with a doctor.
- Don't duplicate what other hospitals or agencies provide. Fill in the gaps and help people to access what is available elsewhere.
- Use trained volunteers and non-professionally qualified staff to do many important tasks under close supervision.
- Keep accurate records of everything you do so you can see what is happening, plan ahead, spot new needs, and are able to communicate with government and donors about the need and what you are doing.
- The work can be spiritually and emotionally draining, so keep close to God, pray together each day as a team and try to create a loving, caring family atmosphere for all who visit.

4. Community teams linked to hospitals – the Salvation Army, Zambia

Sometimes there are huge advantages in making a community care team part of the outreach of a large hospital, such as the Salvation Army hospital at Chikankata. They began ward- and clinic-based HIV work in 1985 with the encouragement of Dr Ian Campbell, the Salvation Army's international health consultant.

Chikankata started specialist AIDS wards, clinics and prevention services, but soon realised the needs were too great and too urgent. In 1987 they started home-care teams linked to hospital diagnosis, counselling, education and treatment. These teams include community nurses, nutritionists and counsellors. They soon expanded into counselling, schools prevention education, child support and technical assistance to other organisations.

The hospital was so large and well equipped that communities tended to look to Chikankata to solve problems, instead of to themselves. There was a lack of community-based healthcare. The original model with professionally trained teams was unable to reach enough people. So they began to invest in less formal teams, run by local communities, providing basic care and bringing people into hospital or to clinics or to the attention of professionally trained staff workers as needed.

Care and prevention teams: lessons learned

- Communities should choose their own team members.
- Local teams can address general development issues, as well as health issues.

- Community teams can help with planning services required (hospitals, clinics, schools, etc.) and how resources are used (people, land, finance).
- Business men and women, teachers and members of community-based organisations should be used to strengthen teams.
- Local churches are often most effective when they seek to serve the whole community.
- Hospital staff can provide help as team members.

5. Flexible models of home care – ACET UK

Community care teams go through many stages of development. Here is a 15-year story in just a few sentences about a team that became a model for others in many nations and then closed itself down.

Pioneer for AIDS began in my own home in London in 1987, working with 50 church volunteers to support people with HIV and AIDS in their homes. In our first year we received considerable support and guidance from World in Need, who saw what was happening and wanted to help transform this small group into a national and international Christian response to AIDS. ACET (AIDS Care, Education and Training) was formed as a result a few months later.

The volunteer group quickly developed into a multi-disciplinary team, with several nurses, a doctor, a social worker and an administrator. A key aim was to make the team redundant as fast as possible – to build the capacity of government doctors and nurses to address this new challenge. The team decided not to prescribe medicines, but only to offer medical advice to doctors – so they would learn from every

---

Palliative care

Palliative care improves the quality of life of people and their families facing life-threatening illness, giving attention to physical, emotional, social and spiritual needs.

Palliative care is an essential part of caring for people living with AIDS because of the variety of symptoms, such as pain, diarrhoea, cough, shortness of breath, nausea, weakness, fatigue, fever and confusion. Palliative care not only relieves symptoms but also reduces visits to the hospital or clinic.

Source: WHO

patient. For the same reasons the team decided not to take over full nursing care, but to support, train, equip and encourage government community nurses. ACET nurses did not wear uniforms, to make it clear that their role was mainly advisory. Another reason was so that neighbours would not guess an AIDS diagnosis.

Every person at home was given a telephone number so they could contact the team any time, day or night, 365 days a year. This was one of the most important parts of the service. Each team member took turns to take the phone home at night or over weekends. They also took home with them enough information about each person to be able to respond to any call in the right way.

If people were very sick, volunteers would stay in their homes on a continuous basis if needed, in shifts of up to eight hours, until the moment of death. They also supported others at home – emotionally as well as practically.

Careful records were kept for each patient. These records and networking were very important as volunteers would often be co-ordinating visits and other support from up to 10 different agencies or individuals.

Suspicion and opposition turns to favour and acceptance

Most of those with HIV in London are men who have sex with men. This community has been very active since 1981, providing counselling and support services. Their experience was that many churches were very hostile to men who were attracted to other men (regardless of whether or not they were sexually active). For this reason, they were concerned that when ACET started, the home-care service might be intolerant, judgemental, unkind or moralistic. They were concerned about hidden motives, thinking that maybe some staff or volunteers might only be interested in recruiting new members for the church.

The people who were looked after by the team became their best supporters – ringing up their friends to tell them about the programme, recommending it to those running HIV clinics and other services. The team became the largest non-government provider of HIV home care across the city.

Government agencies quickly recognised the vital role that the team were playing, that care standards were very high, truly unconditional and available to all, and that clients were included in discussions about what was provided. They then started to fund the work. After the first couple of years, most of the income for ACET home care across the country was coming from government.

Closing the London team to help Africa and Asia

After 12 years, the situation in London changed. Antiviral therapy meant people were living a lot longer with HIV, while government services also improved. After much prayer and reflection, in consultation with other agencies, the team closed down in order to allow resources to be directed to much needier community care teams in Africa and Asia.

At around the same time, all the different ACET care and prevention teams in different nations were given full independence, responsible to their own national boards. The result was a far greater sense of ownership by local churches, lower management costs, faster decisions, greater flexibility, closer relationships with government and local donor agencies, better staff recruitment, big open doors for national influence, and faster, more sustainable growth.

From one small group of volunteers in London, ACET had developed into a rapidly growing, self-sustaining and reproducing, international movement of Christian men and women, responding to HIV in many nations.

ACET UK: lessons learned

- Start small with what you have – a few volunteers is fine.
- Use volunteers who are able to relate naturally and easily to the kind of people you are trying to help.
- Believe that God can do amazing things.
- Bear in mind that sometimes small organisations need to change name and structure to achieve greater things.
- Understand that partnership is key – not just for funding but also to strengthen leadership.
- Invest time in developing key people.
- Adapt rapidly to new needs and opportunities.
- Remember that books, magazines, articles, websites and literature can attract huge donors in unexpected ways.
- Expect your model to be reproduced in other areas, but always adapted in unique ways.
- Do not try to over-control different teams – give them freedom to develop in their situations.

- Be the best you can be – great projects are very unusual and shine like stars.
- Be professional in your approach, efficient and well organised, and you will impress the government.
- Always measure what you do, and provide clear reports to donors and those you have contracts with.
- Persevere if you find that other agencies with different worldviews are trying to attack you, but always listen carefully to their concerns, and be very quick to change what you do if their criticism is justified.
- Try to do yourselves out of a job – make your team redundant and be flexible about your own role.
- Be ready to close down a programme that may still be useful but is not essential any more.
- Pray for wisdom and courage to make the difficult decisions.

6. Adapting the model to support injecting drug users

Another ACET team started in 1988 in Dundee, Scotland, some 450 miles north, with a similar model, adapted to a different situation. It began with 30 volunteers led by June Gray, a church worker and trained nurse. She was worried about the number of injecting drug users in the city. With encouragement from her pastor, she trained a small group of volunteers from her own church, and soon volunteers from other churches started to get involved.

Requests for help grew rapidly, often as drug-using friends introduced others. Many of them were unknown to the authorities and the ACET team was their only source of help. There were many challenges. For example, how can you die at home if you have no home? Homelessness was a major challenge, and the team was soon working with local agencies to find accommodation, and to persuade landlords to rent to people who may not have been reliable at paying rent in the past.

After a while, the project was offered some apartments to manage. It did this so well that more accommodation followed. The team has adapted to each situation – and a major part of the work has been looking after very vulnerable people in special accommodation in various Scottish cities.

The team also started going into schools, providing a comprehensive sexual health education and drugs-prevention programme. It also worked with drug users in the city, to try to prevent the sharing of unsterile injecting equipment, and this became a new focus. The team is known today as Positive Steps. It works across the country in schools, and in Dundee with community support of various kinds.

7. Adapting to UK asylum-seekers

Yet another UK team started in Newcastle, once again adapting the original ACET model. In that region are many women who have arrived in the UK as asylum-seekers from African nations. Quite a few have HIV, are unwell and have very young children. Many of the women have terrible emotional scars from violent attacks on their families back home, killings, rapes and other traumatic experiences. The Newcastle team (now known as Blue Sky Trust) facilitates groups of these women, meeting to support each other, as well as providing help at home, or helping them find places to live.

8. Mobilising churches for home care – TAIP, Uganda

In all these different models – whether in Africa, Asia or Europe – a common element has been mobilising churches. TAIP in Uganda has a particular focus on this vital activity.

Members of the Deliverance Church in Jinja formed a group to offer physical and spiritual care to people with HIV with the support of their pastor, Sam Mugote. Other churches soon saw the positive impact on the lives of individuals, the community and the church itself, and wanted to join in or to start similar programmes. The church set up The AIDS Intervention Programme (TAIP) to support these new church projects.

TAIP teams start with an initial visit to a church to meet with the pastor, church leadership team and interested members of the congregation. It is important that the leadership not only agrees to the programme but is also actively involved. It is their own project, part of the mission of the church. TAIP just provides support and facilitation.

Mobilisation of a whole church typically takes 6 to18 months. Volunteers need to be selected, trained, supported and supervised for their first home visits. TAIP also assists with the ongoing support of volunteers with regular meetings.

Volunteer-based projects often develop faster in rural areas, where people may have more time and can be more flexible about when they are available. In urban areas, family structures are often weaker, and there can be greater work pressures. That means using more paid staff.

The following Bible texts are used by TAIP.

Called to care: 2 Corinthians 1:3–4: 'Comfort those in any trouble with the comfort we ourselves have received from God.' **Example of Jesus**: Mark 1:40–45: 'Filled with compassion, Jesus touched the leper.' **Call to advocacy**: Isaiah 1:17: 'Seek justice, rescue the oppressed, defend the orphan, plead for the widow'. **Call to be non-judgemental**: John 8:2–11: 'If anyone is without sin, let him throw the first stone.' **Call to serve practically and sacrificially**: Luke 10:25–37: the story of the Good Samaritan. **Call to pray**: Ephesians 3:14–21: Paul prays 'that out of God's glorious riches he may strengthen you with power through his Spirit in your inner being'.

Summary on church mobilisation

- Churches often represent huge untapped resources.
- Many members have talents, energy and leadership skills which are not fully used in existing church roles.
- Some church members may be ahead of their leaders in passion, commitment and understanding of HIV, but clear, public leadership support and accountability is vital for rapidly growing, sustainable work.
- Team members need to be living examples of Christ-like compassion and living as they enter homes or schools – they are ambassadors of the programme.
- Available volunteer time may be less in urban areas.

9. Testing of church congregations – Jos, Nigeria

Church mobilisation often goes hand in hand with encouraging congregations to be tested for HIV, especially in countries like Nigeria.

In Plateau State, Nigeria, the government aims to test the entire population for HIV (over 4 million people). It encourages people to find out about their status, so they can then access free treatment.

Many church-based organisations have been talking with church leaders, encouraging them to be tested themselves and in turn to encourage their own leadership teams and congregations to do the same.

How NOT to do HIV testing at church!

'A group asked me if they could come to the church one Sunday morning to talk about AIDS and encourage church members to be tested.

At the end of their message, they asked all those who wanted to be tested to get up out of their seats and go to the back of the church. Several hundred people did so. They were told they would be tested immediately and could come back in an hour or two for their results. They were each asked if they wanted their result to be public or private. Most people did not really understand why it mattered – many are poorly educated and illiterate – and said their results could be made public.

As soon as testing was complete, a man stood up in the church with a long list and started reading out in a loud voice all the names of those who had been tested, and if they were infected with HIV or not. One woman almost fainted when she heard the news in front of the whole church that she was positive. People were very shocked. A woman was driven out by other women who were saying that she was a prostitute because she had HIV. It was really terrible what happened. I know testing is important, but I want to warn people always to offer personal counselling before testing and after testing, and always to keep the results private. Let people who have HIV tell others they trust, and only when they are ready to do so.'

Pastor, Central Nigeria, 2008

ACET Nigeria has been involved in this. The impact can be huge and immediate. Churches are prepared in advance by helping them set up leadership structures for care and support. Such churches become highly motivated to help slow down the further spread of HIV, taking health messages to schools, colleges, offices, farm workers and all other parts of their communities.

Great care needs to be taken, however, when HIV testing on a large scale. Every person needs personal counselling before and after a test, and confidentiality is vital.

Church testing for HIV – lessons learned

- Testing is a vital part of HIV care and prevention.
- Testing should only happen after counselling.
- All those who receive test results should also receive counselling, so that they fully understand what the result means, and are able to think about the implications for them personally.
- Confidentiality of test results is essential to win trust, and each

person's own decision about who they wish to tell and when they wish to tell them should be respected.

- Test results can create huge pastoral issues for church leaders – for example, where a husband tests positive and the wife is negative.
- Positive test results enable people to access treatment as soon as it is available, which may prolong life significantly.
- Positive test results enable those who have HIV to take steps to protect other people.
- Negative test results are usually a huge relief and can encourage people to take action so that they remain negative.
- Positive tests in pregnant women allow a short course of antiviral therapy to be given to protect the unborn child.
- When many people in a church get tested over a short period of time, it means that those who have recently tested positive are not alone: if they wish, they can be helped to link up with others who are positive.
- People may not be able or willing to travel to hospital to be tested, so testing people in the community can be an important way forward. They may trust community teams more than hospitals to keep their results private.

These then are just a very few examples of a huge variety of ways that individual Christians have been deeply touched by HIV and have felt called to make a difference together in the community. They started with just the resources at hand, and have been joined by others who caught the same vision, and their caring work has grown.

A key part of caring is fighting stigma and rejection of people living with HIV – and this has to start inside the church.

CHAPTER SEVEN

POINTING THE FINGER – FIGHTING STIGMA

So what should we think about AIDS, HIV and all these related issues as Christians? I am writing these words while visiting church projects in Nigeria, in parts of the beautiful, hot and dusty countryside where up to 25 per cent of the population are infected with HIV, yet many church leaders are unsure of how to respond. Across the nation as a whole, there are 100 million people who know very little about HIV.

The church in Nigeria is growing. It is deeply traditional in its belief about sexual behaviour, and faces urgent challenges. As in many other nations, a lot of church leaders have struggled to reconcile Sunday preaching messages with the hidden reality: relationship breakdown, sexually active young people and HIV in their own congregations. How should we respond? What words should we use? How do we overcome cultural barriers? How do we fight ignorance, fear, stigma and rejection?

Finding the way of Jesus

HIV work can be really upsetting, stressful and disturbing. It often brings you face to face with a broken, complicated world where no option seems comfortable or quite right. It is often easier to walk away, but the Good Samaritan stopped to get involved.

It is so easy to be an armchair critic, and to quote one Bible verse after another. It is so easy to stand back, tell everyone else exactly how you think the country should be run, or what HIV workers should do, preach nice sermons from pulpits, and make bold theological statements. It is so easy to visit people in neat hospital beds. They easily become numbers, cases and statistics.

What would Jesus do? I often hear those words. 'Jesus would never

113

Teaching in the church

'Since the training week I attended, people in my church are willing to hear about HIV and AIDS because I use the Bible as my reference – Jesus caring for the needy and God warning the people through the prophet Ezekiel. I also show them love.

Some people say that AIDS is not real. Or that AIDS in their bodies is not really happening. Some also dispute the results of their HIV tests if they test positive after going to the hospital. They say things like, "I reject that result in the name of Jesus!" They cannot accept it. Maybe they are expecting instant healing.

Many in my church did the test after I explained why it mattered for them to know their status. One thing which helped me start the AIDS programmes in my church was the teaching I was given, about not discriminating against or stigmatising those who are infected. By God's grace I will now go and give a seminar on AIDS to 1,000 people in my regional church association, encouraging them to receive counselling and testing for HIV and to start their own programmes.'

Baptist pastor, Central Nigeria, January 2009

have done that,' people say, sometimes about some aspect of AIDS prevention.

'What would Jesus do?' is a wonderful phrase, and reminds us that we are his disciples, and that in all we do we should live up to his calling. However, there are many things Christians do that we recognise as good, but find very hard to imagine Jesus doing himself. For example, making love to your husband or wife (Jesus was strictly celibate); fighting in an army (yet few Christians are totally pacifist); trading millions of dollars of stocks and shares in a bank every hour (does it fit your Jesus image? Yet many Christians work in banks); being Prime Minister of a country (Jesus refused every opportunity to enter politics or support political parties).

So let us be very careful to be consistent. Jesus is our guide in all things. The words he said bring life, peace, health and wholeness to us. And his Spirit is compassion and love, especially for those who are unloved. But be sure you do not limit Jesus by your own culture or limited understanding. I am sure many of us will be in for a great surprise when we meet him in the next life face to face. His grace is so much greater than ours. His love is total; ours is always limited.

Life is so simple when you don't have to get close to people in desperate need, and to the lives they are forced to lead. And it is easy to judge when you don't really care.

Be very slow to judge

As you judge others, you will one day be judged (Matthew 7:1–2). When you touch 'real life' situations, you may never be quite the same again. So many theologians and Christian thinkers have had to change their opinions when confronted with reality: someone they really care about, in a situation they have never had to face before. I have also been forced to change my own mind on a number of key issues over the last 20 years, as I have learned more about actual situations. I have known church leaders totally shift position when confronted with new situations in their own churches.

When you visit someone at home, you learn more about them in two minutes than you would in 10 years on a hospital ward, in a clinic or in a day centre.

You are instantly touched by their world. Their young children run to you. The cracked mug, the dusty floor, the piles of dirty washing, the overflowing sink and the empty food store may all be signs that she is ill today, tired and needs your help.

She is so relieved that you came as you promised. You have become part of her extended family, a trusted friend, confidant and faithful servant. Today she wants to talk about who will look after her children after she is gone. . . .

I have seen volunteers with tears streaming down their faces, suddenly overwhelmed when they get back to their own homes. Staff who need time out, because yet another much-loved client, or relative, or friend, or staff member has died.

We need to take care of those in the front line, and not judge them. When we draw close to the poorest of the poor, the sick, the marginalised, those who are rejected by society, those whose lives are broken or who are in real trouble, those whose only experience of 'love' is being sexually abused – it can affect us very deeply.

It hurts when you watch someone you love go on making decisions that you know will probably destroy them. It hurts when you are rejected by someone you are trying to help. It hurts when people misunderstand your motives. It hurts to be close to people who themselves are hurting very much in their own personal lives.

And when they are gone, when you are at the funeral, or with the family some weeks later, sharing in their own sadness, you may know you have made a big difference, but also that you have paid a personal price.

Living as a priest with HIV

Canon Gideon Byamugisha is a 50-year-old Ugandan Anglican priest with HIV. His first wife died of AIDS and he has since married another woman with HIV. He is co-founder of INERELA+, an international network of religious leaders – lay and ordained, women and men – living with, or personally affected by, HIV. INERELA+ was born out of the African network ANERELA+.

I am one of the millions of casualties of the silence surrounding sex and sexuality. The first time I heard about condoms was the day I received my positive result. It was after my wife died in 1991, yet I should have had an HIV test before I was married in 1987.

I decided to break the silence and disclose my status for two reasons. One was actually personal in the sense that I felt that if I talked about my situation then people would be in a better position to support me with accurate information, with the services for self-protection and also self-care. But the other one was more of a religious leadership responsibility. I felt that if I lived a double identity, then I would not be giving a model example to the people I lead, knowing that I'm one thing in public and another thing in private.

Integrating HIV in the daily life of a parish church means that you ensure that during your service and ministry in the church, you strive to give people accurate information about HIV; you strive to change their attitudes both to the disease and to people living with it; you strive to build their skills in self-protection and self-care; you try to ensure that they have the best services that can help protect them and their loved ones, like voluntary counselling and testing, like post-test clubs where they meet for sharing information and positive living; and we also create a supportive environment that promotes gaining solidarity against HIV.'

Source: interviews on ABC Radio, 26 July 2006, and in the Independent, *11 July 2000*

Sickness and suffering can be hard to understand

Life can seem very unfair. It can be hard to understand why God allows things to happen the way they do.

The story of Job tells us that God allows suffering and sickness to happen to those who love him (Job 1), but also that he comes to strengthen us at such times. Paul also encourages us to understand that sufferings of various kinds help us to endure, develop our character and cause us to hope (Romans 5:3).

Paul also tells us that through our own experience of suffering, we are able to offer comfort to others in similar situations. We can share the hope we ourselves receive from God (2 Corinthians 1:3–7). If we do not know what it is like in various tough situations, how can we help others?

What about physical healing through prayer?

Most Christians believe that God has the power to heal – after all, he created the whole world, and the Bible reminds us that Jesus healed many people. A few leaders even teach that it is not God's will for any Christian to be sick.

But we need to face the reality that there is a huge amount of sickness inside churches and in the wider community, despite many prayers. And each one of us gets older and less healthy every day.

Of course God can heal people with different medical problems whenever he wants. Amazing things can happen that astound doctors. However, believers and pastors can easily make fatal mistakes. They are not doctors, so how can they be 100 per cent sure the person is really healed? They may feel God has told them, but the apostle Paul warns us that we all see only through a veil. Even he was limited in knowledge. We know in part and can only prophesy in part (1 Corinthians 13:9–12).

Church leaders can bring harm

Such mistakes can easily mean HIV spreads faster. Some people have been encouraged by others in their churches to stop taking antiviral treatment in the belief that they have already been healed. This is extremely dangerous. Really serious errors are made in ignorance every day about whether people have been healed or not, by respected senior church leaders who have great faith and integrity. While we can certainly pray for healing, anyone who believes they may have received healing should first be re-tested for HIV. If they have really been healed, they should now test negative. Let the doctors confirm what has happened.

Please, please be careful. If you tell someone they are healed of HIV, and you are wrong, they may stop using condoms with their husband or wife. You may end up causing the death of their partner and their child too. What if a pregnant woman throws away antiviral medicines that are protecting her unborn baby? Adults may stop treatment and die fast, leaving young orphans.

These are urgent matters of life and death. We are commanded by Jesus to pray for the sick – and to persevere in prayer (Matthew 10:8; Luke 18:1). But pastors *must* do what Jesus did. He told those he had cured of leprosy to go to the priests (the medical experts at the time) to confirm a cure (Luke 17:14).

HIV can be confusing

Illnesses related to HIV can be confusing. People often get better before becoming ill again – even without much medical help. I remember a particular event shortly after ACET started home care in London. One of our London volunteers came back after a visit to provide practical care to a man who had been very ill in bed, and who was expected to die quite soon. He looked very shocked. 'What's happened?' I asked. He told me that when he arrived, he found his client was out of bed, up a tall ladder, full of energy, mending the roof! The client continued to be very active for several weeks, then got another chest infection and died peacefully at home with those he loved around him.

When people with AIDS suddenly get better for a while, they often think that what helped them is a miracle of God, or some traditional herbal remedy that they took the day before. This is how many false 'cure' stories begin.

Mistakes also stop people getting pastoral support. I have seen very sick men and women with various diseases only days from death, while their church leaders are boasting about them being living demonstrations of the miraculous power of God – even though it is obvious to their doctors that they are very likely to die soon.

Comfort and support the sick – do not accuse

Some people with HIV do not want to disappoint those who are praying for them, who are still convinced (against all evidence) that they have been healed or will be. Sometimes sick people put on brave faces for pastors, hiding the truth from all except close friends and family. I get very upset if people in the church suggest that the reason someone is not healed is because of the sick person's own lack of faith, or lack of holiness. What a terrible burden to load onto the back of someone who needs comfort and support! Then people start blaming themselves for their own lack of faith as the reason they have not experienced a miracle. Faith in God should be a comfort, not cause a crisis.

Timothy continued to be unwell despite many prayers and was told by Paul to take care of himself – he was not told to repent because of his lack of faith (1 Timothy 5:23). Paul himself continued to live with a 'thorn in the flesh' despite many prayers (2 Corinthians 12:7). Care of the sick has always been part of the Christian tradition. Missionaries established hospitals and clinics all over the world. They accepted then that God calls us to use medicines to heal the sick; that prayer is part of our calling but not the total answer.

Sometimes test results may be confusing. Two different types of test are needed to confirm HIV. Usually both are done together, but sometimes people are given the first test result only (which can be confused by other infections), and are only given the result from the second test two weeks later. This may lead to mistaken claims of healing if people are given a negative result first, and then a positive result from the second test. If there is any doubt, tests should be repeated. 'Instant' tests use three different methods to detect HIV infection – and even they can sometimes (rarely) give a wrong result. (For more on testing accuracy see page 66.)

Practical care with a soft heart

Someone once said to me that she was shocked that Christians were involved in compassionate, unconditional care for people with HIV, because her understanding was that we disapproved of many of the lifestyles that had caused people to become infected.

She had confused agreeing with caring. They have never been the same thing in medicine. If a doctor only looked after people who voted for the same party, who held the same faith or who worshipped in the same kind of church, they would be struck off the medical register right away.

Doctors and nurses are expected to give good compassionate care to all who need it and for all illnesses, regardless of how people come to be ill. The same is true for all those involved in the so-called caring professions.

In the same way, Christians who are only prepared to look after

Voices of people living with HIV

'You look at me, and you see a healthy woman. You can shake my hand, drink from my glass, even embrace me. . . None of these things will give you HIV. There were times when I was abandoned and alone because even my closest friends and family turned away from me. They did not understand these things.'

Source: www.globalaidsalliance.org

'If someone in a village falls on hard times, their neighbours are always there to help. But this is not the case if someone has HIV. If a community member becomes ill with HIV, she is shunned by everyone. The only way to fight this problem is through education. When people understand the disease and learn that they can safely offer help and support to their family and neighbours who are sick, then they will begin to do what is right.'

Source: www.globalaidsalliance.org

'I have lost a lot because of HIV, but I have gained so much more. We must work together to fight the stigma and ignorance surrounding this disease, but perhaps even more importantly, we should learn to help each other and not turn our backs on other women and mothers who need help and support.'

Djama Amadou, HIV-positive woman in Niger

Source: 'A Shining Example: Living with HIV in Niger', CARE International, August 2006

'I earned a living for this family. I earned money to send my younger sisters and brothers to school, for them to graduate and live like other young people do. Now I was the one bringing shame on the family, humiliating my younger sisters. Why did I get this? Was it my fault? Whatever it was, they called me "the AIDS woman". And they said it like a new swear word.'

Anonymous
Source: 'The AIDS Woman', ACRE International, November 2006

certain groups of people with HIV should either be asked to leave HIV care projects or helped to change their views over time (avoid using them in direct caring roles initially). When we started ACET home care in London we asked every volunteer a question: Who would you have more sympathy for – a woman who got HIV as a commercial sex worker, a man who has had sex with other men, someone who got it through a blood transfusion, someone who was a drug user or a baby infected in the womb and so on.

Those who had harsh attitudes to some kinds of people were not accepted onto the programme unless they were willing to reconsider their attitudes. And we needed to be certain that they really had experienced a deep change in their hearts. People cannot give wonderful care if they are burning up inside. Our care must be unconditional, offered to all regardless of how they came to be affected by HIV. When a volunteer goes into a home, they represent the entire organisation, they are an ambassador on behalf of the church, as well as the HIV project. They are part of our family, extending that sense of family to all we care for.

Pointing the finger is the easy way out

Negative attitudes to people with HIV can help the virus spread faster. If people are afraid to talk about it, prevention becomes more difficult. It is also harder to encourage those at risk to go for testing if they are afraid of being rejected. But that means they don't get treated, and also that they may continue without realising it to spread HIV to others. We need to create a supportive and caring environment if we are to have any real hope of controlling the spread of HIV in future.

Many illnesses are caused by lifestyles that some would question: should we have any sympathy for a man who has smoked 50 cigarettes a day for the last 40 years and now has lung cancer? What about a young girl who falls and breaks her leg at a party because she has had too much to drink? What about an overweight man who has a heart attack or a stroke?

At the end of the day it is easier to blame people and have nothing to do with them. It is a neat and tidy way of making it someone else's problem. You don't have to feel guilty about not getting involved, because in your own mind you have made someone else guilty. It is the same mentality as that of a very wealthy man who told me recently that he did not want to help the starving, because they would only need more food during the next drought.

Cause and effect

AIDS is *not* the judgment of God and it never was. HIV was *not* created by him as a tool to punish the world. If it was, God's judgment must be remarkably selective. What about babies infected in the womb or through medical treatments?

AIDS is just another in a long series of diseases which can be spread by sex. Sex is an easy, even lazy, way for a disease to spread and this is the way HIV usually spreads.

Any doctor knows that the majority of illnesses they see could probably be avoided or reduced if people lived differently – even something as simple as washing hands before eating. The whole of health education is showing people cause and effect. If you smoke, you damage your lungs. If you drive when you are high on drugs, you are likely to drive off the road and kill someone. If you get drunk, you will have a hangover and can damage your liver. If you inject using a contaminated needle, you can get hepatitis or HIV. If you eat too much, you can get heart disease. *You reap what you sow*, as we read in 2 Corinthians 9:6.

Cause and effect is the most important lesson we have to learn as children. When you were young, your parents probably told you a hundred times a day to come away from something, or to put something down, for your own safety. Your mother probably then explained to you, for example, that a pan of boiling water is extremely hot and if you touch it with your fingers, you will burn yourself.

None of us is very good at listening at first. Usually there are one or two near disasters, followed by: 'I told you so. Now when I tell you next time, you'll do exactly what I say.' And then we learn.

Our loving Father

The Bible says that God is a loving Father. Because he loves us, he looks on us as his children. He cares about each person as if that person is the only person in the whole world. Because he cares for us that much he wants to help us and to protect us from our own mistakes. But he respects you as a person and he will never dominate your life. He is always there ready and waiting to help you, but you must ask. He will never impose himself. Nor will he ever go away. You can turn your back on him for years, but he is always there ready and waiting with open arms. There is nothing that you can do that can put you outside his love for you, although you can keep your distance from him, with consequences both here and in the next life.

I often think of the story Jesus told about the Prodigal Son (Luke 15). The son had a disagreement with his father and wanted to go off to the city and do his own thing. He found living on his own was terrible. He had a really hard time. He spent all his money on trying to have a great time and then found himself feeding pigs in a field. He kept wondering if his dad would accept him again. He was tired, upset, hungry and lonely.

He reckoned that even if his dad wouldn't accept him back as a member of the family, he would prefer to go home on any terms – even as a servant. When he was almost home he got nervous, but his dad saw him coming from a distance and rushed out to meet him. The son felt ashamed and wouldn't even look up, but his father flung his arms around him and swept him into the house, cancelled all his arrangements and threw a great coming home party, much to the disgust of the older son.

Jesus told the story to show us that God's love never goes cold or goes away, just because we go far away from God. God wants you to know how to avoid the pain of your mistakes, and how to live a happy, full and satisfying life. The Bible is full of examples of cause and effect. In fact you could say it is one of the main teachings of the Bible.

Sexual behaviour, relationships and the traditional teachings of the church

Around a third of all adults alive today would say they are Christians – the largest religion in the world.[1] Most Christians today live in Africa, Latin America, the former Soviet bloc and South-east Asia. They are often very passionate about what they believe, and are reaching out into their communities, seeing new members added every week.

The contrast could not be greater with North America, Western Europe, Australia and New Zealand, where attendance in many churches has been in decline for some decades, particularly in parts of the church where views are likely to be less traditional and more liberal. For example, some leaders of liberal churches have questioned whether Jesus really did miracles, whether he really did rise physically from the dead, whether what the Bible says is true, and whether Christians still need to follow 'out of date' teachings about sexual behaviour that were written 2,000 years ago.

---

[1] *World Christian Encyclopaedia*, 2001 Edition

Almost all rapidly growing churches around the world (particularly in countries hit hardest by HIV) are very traditional in their core beliefs about Jesus, lifestyles and personal discipline in sexuality. They preach a clear message of life-changing faith that includes abstinence outside of marriage and faithfulness within – values that seem even more important in a world where HIV has infected so many.

These same values have been taught in all church denominations for almost all of the last 2,000 years, and are based on the Bible – in particular on the words of Jesus himself.

Of course, we need to read the Bible very carefully to understand what the whole of it says about life, not just pulling out a sentence or two. You can easily read bits of phrases here and there and string them out to mean whatever you want them to. The overall meaning is vitally important. We also need to think about the people at the time, to whom certain things were written, their local situation and culture, and how the passage fits together with other parts of the Bible. Then we are in a better position to understand the lessons for us today.

The most widely accepted interpretation of what the Bible says about relationships is that which has been handed down from one generation to another over 2,000 years. The Bible teaches right from the start that God made man and woman in his own image (Genesis 1:24). His intention is that a man should marry a woman, and that sex is to be a wonderful gift, a mystery uniting a man and woman who have committed themselves to each other in this way for life. God created sex: it was his idea. Jesus made it absolutely clear that he agreed with the established teaching, which was that sex outside marriage was wrong. In fact he went further, to say that even to have a fantasy about sex outside marriage was wrong (Matthew 5:28).

Out of that kaleidoscope of rich physical love are to come children who grow up in a secure loving family, with grannies and grandpas, aunts and uncles, cousins, and single people included in family life if they want.

This teaching about abstinence outside of marriage, and faithfulness within, is not the tradition of one denomination but of all Christian denominations, whether Catholic, Eastern Orthodox, Anglican, Methodist or whatever. In fact it is one of the few things about which Christians over the centuries have always united.

Abstinence from sexual relationships outside of marriage and faithfulness within is also the teaching of Islam, Judaism, Hinduism and many other religions. That is the reason why very different faith-based groups often share very similar approaches to HIV prevention, especially when educating young people.

There are many problems in societies today. Many of these can be linked to the breakdown of families and communities. A lot of vandalism, alcohol problems, drug problems, teenage psychological problems and other situations can be traced to the unhappy homes of the young people concerned.

Marriage is seen by all world religions as the basic foundation stone of society. Where marriages break down, where there is violence in the home, or where spouses cheat on each other and stop caring, then children often grow up with deep scars, insecure and unsure of themselves.

The Bible, by encouraging everything that supports a good stable marriage, speaks out against anything that undermines marriage as the rock on which society is built.

Stretching the limits

The Bible teaches that people can be sexually aroused in a great number of different situations. It is very explicit. It talks about men having sex with men, adults having sex with children, men having sex with their mothers, people having sex with animals, the rape of women and men, orgies, sexual favours in exchange for money or food, and many other things. All of these different types of sexual act that take place outside of a marriage between a man and a woman are mentioned in the Bible, but always as something beyond God's ideal for us.

The Bible also describes very close, warm, intense, loving, committed relationships between people of the same sex: Ruth and Naomi or David and Jonathan, for example. David and Jonathan could share as much of their lives together as they liked, but they could not indulge in same-sex activity without breaking the rules God had given. Once again, these basic rules for sexual behaviour are common to most world religions.

However, whatever our own personal views may be, we must remember that in every situation, the Bible teaches us that we are called to have deep love for *all* people, regardless of any other factor – including sexual preferences, temptations, lifestyles or differences of opinion about interpretations of Christian teaching (Matthew 5:44; John 3:16). For this we need God's help and grace.

Called to love friends, family, strangers – even enemies

This teaching of love is central to the message of Jesus, yet I am shocked at how intolerant, cruel and insensitive some Christians can be, especially when it comes to issues like HIV or relationships between people of the same sex. It is easy to have double standards, and to be a hypocrite in the sight of God, denying the teachings of Jesus himself.

Take, for example, a church with traditional teachings that welcomes men who come home drunk several times every month and beat their wives. Or one that welcomes a man and woman who are not married but are in a sexual relationship; or a man who gambles his wages and fails to take care of his family. Yet the same church may be very unfriendly towards two men or two women who are in a sexual relationship.

Jesus told us that love for friends is not enough. Love for our neighbour is not enough. Love for those who are different from us in culture or belief is not enough. Love for those we strongly disagree with is not enough. Jesus told us that the true test of our love is when we love even our enemies: those who hate us, those who oppose us, those who persecute us, those we find it humanly impossible to love. Those are the people we are called to love also. That kind of love is the sign of God's Spirit at work in us.

Indeed we are not just to show deep, compassionate, caring love, but also to pray to God for his blessing on such people. 'But I say to you, *Love* your enemies, *bless* them that curse you, *do good* to them that hate you, and *pray* for them which spitefully use you, and persecute you' (Matthew 5:44).[2]

Loving and caring – does it mean agreeing also?

People confuse loving and agreeing. We are called to love all people just as Jesus loves all people. When he lived on earth, Jesus himself often had strong disagreements with people about life, belief, attitudes and so on, but he still loved them. In the same way, we are not called to force ourselves somehow to agree with everything people think or do.

---

[2] American King James Version

Some people may say: 'How can you love me and accept me as a person if you cannot approve of all the decisions I make and of the way I choose to live?' But this just shows that they have a very limited view of love. It would mean it is not possible for a human being to love someone who votes for a different political party, or who follows a different religion, or who has a different lifestyle.

I love my children – even if as adults they do things I would prefer they did not do, or I think may be unwise (happily this is very rarely the case). I will still go on loving them, even if I think they might be making a mistake. And I hope they will still love me too, even though I am imperfect in so many ways.

So then, God calls us to be compassionate to *all*, supporting people in *all* the different personal challenges they may face, in their longings, challenges, pressures, temptations, frustrations and pain. God calls us to repent of our own harshness, intolerance, judgmental attitudes and cynical pride. To repent of our lack of care and rejection of those who feel differently. To repent of the way in which we as Christians have often stigmatised those with HIV.

Celibacy has always been seen as a high calling

We think in this sex-dominated age that for a man (or in some cultures also for a woman) not to express their sexuality by having sex with another person is somehow against the laws of nature and is wrong.

Christian tradition has always given high honour to those who are celibate. Jesus himself is our supreme example and the apostle Paul. Celibacy has always been seen as a high calling for leaders in the church and has continued in monastic communities – monks, nuns and friars – as well as in the Catholic priesthood, and among Eastern and Oriental Orthodox bishops. Celibacy is a high calling in other religions too – for example, Buddhist monks.

In many parts of the church total commitment to Christ and celibacy have gone together. Of course temptations can come to break celibacy vows, but the fact is that sexual abstinence has been a central part of Christian leadership traditions.

The time of the early church was also a culture obsessed with sexual fulfilment and immorality, and both Jesus and Paul spoke out clearly in favour of temperance, discipline, self-control, celibacy and faithfulness as part of God's purpose for us all. In the next century people will look perhaps with some amusement at the first and second generation who grew up with the pill, the obsession with sex, and the domination of sexually transmitted infections. Sadly they will also record the devastation of family break-up on hundreds of millions of children.

Our mission and calling

In many countries you will find churches at the very forefront of HIV care and prevention. Churches are doing this in the same tradition of compassionate, professional healthcare and education that established so many tens of thousands of hospitals, clinics and schools across Africa and Asia over the last 100 years.

Church-based institutions have formed part of the backbone of health provision in many nations for decades. They remain a significant, trusted and reliable force. In most places, existing church programmes and Christian healthcare programmes have been extended or adapted to include HIV.

Churches are not only providing loving support for those affected by HIV, and saving lives, but are also challenging oppression and fighting injustice, victimisation, prejudice and rejection.

They are fighting for equal access to treatment for all with HIV, and doing all they can to encourage acceptance of those with HIV and their families. And they are welcoming those with HIV into the community of the church, supporting them with friendship and love, recognising at the same time that there are often many complex pastoral and spiritual issues to work through.

These things are our mission, our God-given calling, and we can do nothing else.

So then, we have looked at many ways to prevent HIV, to support those affected, to fight stigma and show compassion. We need now to look at issues of life and death – in particular attitudes towards sickness and dying that can make life more difficult for those living with HIV, and for those who support them.

CHAPTER EIGHT

ISSUES OF LIFE AND DEATH

Worse than cancer

Imagine being told at the age of 23 that you have cancer and cannot be cured. Your whole world has fallen apart in an instant: all your hopes and dreams for the future have been dashed. It cannot really be true. It is hard to take in: your plans for training, a job, a home of your own, maybe to get married and have children, and live to a ripe old age – all of these things have been crushed.

But when the diagnosis is an illness related to HIV it can seem far worse. Sometimes I ask a class at school what they would do if they went to give blood and a few days later a letter came asking them to re-attend. When they go back they are told their blood has tested positive for HIV. Many people tell me they would commit suicide rather than face the thought of life with HIV. This is why so much care and support is needed after someone has been told.

A friend of mine who is a doctor was shocked one day to wake up in the morning and find that someone had parked his car at the back of his house and had gassed himself with the exhaust. He had discharged himself against advice from the hospital just a few hours previously. He could not face the thought of life with HIV.

I do not believe there is anywhere in the world where people with HIV have not experienced rejection, hostility, prejudice and fear.

An increasing number of church leaders are becoming ill from HIV, particularly in Africa (see page 71). Of course the first question many people want answered when they meet a church leader with HIV is how they got it. And they may change their opinion of the person as soon as they find out.

Many church leaders with HIV were infected before they found

faith in Christ. Ohers have been infected since, through medical treatments or as a result of a sexual relationship with someone who is
living with HIV – in many cases their spouse.

Fighting to survive

People often lose their jobs when the boss finds out why they are ill. In
most parts of the world life is very tough if you cannot earn enough
to feed your family.

A young child may end up looking after her dying mother, after
burying her father, caring for two or three younger brothers and sisters
and trying somehow to get money for food. It is not enough for a community care team to go rushing in and out with a packet of medicines
and a new blanket. Caring for AIDS widows, orphans and vulnerable
children has become a major challenge: helping them rebuild their
lives and find a way to survive long term. Microfinance (small loans)
can help start an income-generating activity, with training, support
and encouragement from the local church. Children in child-led
households often need to be taught basic skills such as how to repair a
leaking roof in a mud-brick hut, or how to look after the goat. These
are all vital expressions of practical Christian love.

The best support is usually right there in the community: neighbours, friends, other family members, church members. A kind neighbour who cooks for the children, or an uncle who visits regularly and
brings food; keeping them on their own land, in their own village,
among their own people.

But community support of orphans can often break down, especially
in big cities where most people now live. Community support remains
an ideal but may not always be possible. Each child's situation is totally
unique. Every family group and community is different. There is no one
right or wrong way to support children who have lost parents.

Every day the number of people with financial difficulties
because of HIV is growing. A landlord may object if he discovers
one of his tenants has HIV. Maybe he is afraid the rest will move
out when they get to hear, or maybe have harsh feelings like some of
the others we have seen. Either way, it is quite common for someone
to come out of hospital after just being told they have HIV to
discover their belongings have been thrown out and the locks have
been changed.

Who can be trusted?

For someone who has just learned they have HIV, usually the hardest thing to cope with is the response of the people around them. Will the next person they meet feel sorry for them (which they would hate) or want to see them dead and tell them it's all their own fault? Who is their friend and who is their enemy? If they tell their friend about the illness, will it be kept a secret, or how many days will it take until the friend has told someone else who tells the whole community? The accumulated shock, grief and anguish of losing many relatives and friends because of AIDS can also mean that people run out of energy and inner resources.

No wonder suicide can be seen as a better option.

But there is another way. Churches can be very caring and support-ive places, where people with HIV are fully accepted, loved and cared for. Many congregations have special support groups where people with HIV can meet together to encourage each other, share news and pray. We need to remember, however, that church leaders and doctors have very different roles, and while church leaders can offer great pastoral and emotional support, medical help should also be sought.

All over the world, attitudes are becoming much more positive and accepting of those with HIV. Ignorance and fear are rapidly disap-pearing – even in places where personal risk-taking has yet to change. Widespread HIV testing has made HIV a more normal part of life, as millions more people are discovering they are HIV-positive, and mil-lions of others are relieved to discover that they are not (although they realise they could easily have been).

New treatments have revolutionised the outlook of millions of people with HIV. Someone in Africa just 10 years ago might have been expected to live only five years on average after testing positive for HIV. But today, with earlier testing and better treatment, many people are now enjoying 20 years or more of healthy life after first knowing their positive status.

So HIV has changed from a warning of possible early death to diagnosis of a chronic condition, which can often be managed to allow a relatively normal and active life.

And antiviral treatment also now means that up to 99 babies out of 100 born to mothers with HIV will grow up totally free of the virus, hopefully to lead completely healthy lives.

Life beyond life

However, although new treatments can prolong life for many years, people with HIV do eventually get very sick with AIDS, unless some other condition develops first.

If we are going to look after people who are seriously ill, then we have to come to terms ourselves with what we think about death. Most of us don't like to talk about death. We deny death exists. In some countries children are kept well away from funerals, perhaps because adults are embarrassed to cry in front of them.

It is this fear of death, the fear of the unknown, that is one reason why HIV is so scary. People often ask me how I can spend so much time with people who are dying – it used to be due to cancer, then it was HIV. The answer is because I know where I'm going.

When I had just qualified as a doctor, one of the first patients I had was an old woman who was dying of cancer. I remember sitting on her hospital bed one afternoon and she took my hand. 'You'll remember me when I've gone, won't you?' she said. I nodded and she went on: 'You know where you're going, don't you? You believe?'

I had never said anything to her about faith. I do not carry a label, or a symbol, or a Bible, but she had picked something up. She sensed that I was at peace with her dying. She could see that I was not afraid and that I was not going to abandon her because hope of her cure had abandoned me.

When managed properly, death is almost always a peaceful and dignified thing. Often the relative in the room is not even sure if the person has died or not; he or she just appears to be sleeping.

Death is a mystery

If you have ever had the privilege of sitting with someone at the moment of their death, you have experienced a mystery. Here is a woman bounded by place and time. You are sitting there holding her hand. She is breathing quietly. Most of the time she is asleep, but occasionally she opens her eyes or says a word. She is not in any pain, she is not anxious and she knows exactly what is happening. She is not afraid and is at peace.

As you are sitting there you notice that her breathing has become more laboured, and she seems sleepier. Over what seems like hours, but is in fact a few minutes, the breathing changes again. The nurse comes in and says her pulse is very weak and rapid now. There are small beads of sweat on her brow.

Gradually her breathing seems to fade away, and is gone. You wonder if she has died. After a few minutes you get a shock when she suddenly takes another deep breath before all is quiet again. And after a while you realise she has gone.

At the end of the day it is a mystery. Death heightens spiritual awareness in every way. It is a brave person who watches this mystery, or perhaps watches the birth of a child, and who can walk away convinced there is no spiritual dimension to life.

Four reactions to dying

When you know you are dying, four things start to happen. The first is that your priorities change. What is the point in carrying on with your college course when the doctors have told you that you will probably be dead by Christmas?

The second thing is that it alters your relationships. You find your best friend can't cope and hasn't visited you once in hospital, while someone else has been a real support and nothing is ever too much trouble. Sometimes it takes a life-threatening crisis for people to discover who they really are, and who is important to them.

Thirdly, it can be a time of great regrets. People may find themselves looking back and wondering if they would have done things differently if they had known life was going to be so short.

Finally, people find they are looking forward. Most people I talk to are not so much afraid of death as afraid of the process of dying: they are afraid of becoming incontinent, of losing control, of being in pain, of becoming a burden, of being totally dependent. Afraid of suffocating to death, of being buried while still alive (a common worry), of losing the ability to think, move or remember. Afraid for their young children and who will look after them, love them, protect them. Maybe they are also worried about their old and frail parents, or about their husband or wife.

Deathbed conversion

People who know they are dying can become very sensitive to all spiritual experience, with a growing desire to know God intimately. In their final days they may have vivid dreams of the next life, or tell you that they are seeing visions of angels or other things.

Deathbed conversion is common and very real. The thief on the cross turned to Christ in the act of dying. People will often ask to be prayed for if they know you have faith in God. They may have faith that your prayers will work, even if they sometimes doubt that God exists or are confused about who he is. Prayer and the laying on of hands can be deeply moving and a comforting experience for those who are sick.

Finding inner peace

Sometimes people need to know for the very first time that they really are forgiven by God, and to reach a place in their hearts where they are able to forgive themselves. They may have important final words for close family, responsibilities to formally hand on, instructions they want to give. Only when they have completed all their 'unfinished business' are they able to fully relax and let go, ready to die peacefully.

This is why it is vital to be sensitive to what the person wants. Don't always try to raise their spirits, or pretend they are getting better, when they know themselves deep down that their life is fading away. Often relatives think that their loved one has no idea about how ill they are, so they avoid such conversations ('Please don't tell him, doctor'). Yet as soon as they leave the room the person says to the doctor: 'Please don't tell my wife I am going to die – it will upset her.' People who are dying desperately need to be able to talk openly and honestly. Every moment really matters when you know you have only hours or days or weeks to live. Dying can be a very lonely experience.

Dying can also be a very beautiful thing, surrounded by close family, in the person's own home, where they are comfortable and at peace, ready to pass on to the next life. Every second of every day takes on new meaning, and such special moments will be treasured for many years to come by those who love the person.

When my father died of cancer, we nursed him at home. Every day for six weeks close friends would come for tea in the afternoon and gather round his bed. There was a lot of laughter in the room and many tears. It was a time of celebration of good memories, of sadness, of saying really important things, of expressing love and appreciation, of enjoying the moment, of getting ready to say goodbye. And as each person got up to go, with a final hug there would always be the thought that maybe this was the last time they would meet here on earth.

Often no words need to be said; it is enough just to be there with the person on their final stages of the journey.

More to life than life

As a Christian I believe that there is a life after this one and that death is merely a gateway from a physical world, limited by space and time, to another dimension. Jesus taught quite clearly that when this is all over, each of us will have to give an account of what we have done with our lives.

Jesus also showed us that not one of us is perfect in and of ourselves: none of us can please God (Romans 3:23). None of us is perfect enough to enter his presence and survive. But the good news is that God has bridged that huge gulf between himself and us by sending Jesus. The things that you and I have done wrong have eternal consequences. We're responsible, and the penalty for what we have done is ultimately death and extinction (Romans 6:23).

But God sent Jesus to receive the punishment that should have been ours. By dying for us, Jesus set us free from the effects of our own wrongdoing. Through Jesus, for those who accept him and receive him, God has chosen to forgive us completely and wipe the record completely clean. Through Jesus we call on the unreachable, unknowable, unfathomable God as our Father (John 1:12).

For those who believe, the moment of death is a change from being only partly aware of God and his love, to being fully and completely in his presence, an experience of heaven itself.

A right time and place

This teaching about what happens after death has always been a central part of the church, but immediately raises a question in many people's minds if they hear that churches are becoming involved in providing practical care for people with HIV. Will Christians want to try and preach the gospel to every person they meet who is dying?

A prominent member of an AIDS organisation who had AIDS himself was a convert to Buddhism. He freely admitted with a smile that when he was with people who had HIV, all he really wanted to do was tell them about his faith, but he knew he should not. If he did, then everyone else with different faiths who visited the person would do the same. The person's last days would be pressured from every direction by different carers.

What does the person really want? If someone with HIV asks to see a chaplain, they are asking for spiritual help. If all the chaplain is interested in doing is visiting them at home to do cooking, wash clothes, help with the children and bring water, you can imagine they might well feel disappointed. It is a real privilege to be allowed to be with someone who is approaching the end of their life. People are rightly very sensitive about others visiting people who may be too weak to say 'no' or 'please go away'. Often it is only afterwards that the ill person pleads for a certain person never to visit again. If you are vulnerable, you think twice before possibly offending someone on whom your life could depend.

If a doctor at a government clinic asks a volunteer agency for a community visitor, he expects practical help, not a chaplain. If it gets back that a particular visitor spent their time trying to convert their patient, the doctor may well feel justifiably angry. As far as he is concerned, the community service is completely useless.

It is not a service to him as a doctor because he would be extremely worried about asking anyone else to go in from that group again. It is not a service for the patient because what they wanted was good company and a helping hand, and instead they got a preacher!

The doctor comes to the conclusion that this particular AIDS programme is only interested in trying to convert people. As a doctor, he will campaign to make sure everyone knows about these religious activists.

Guest and servant

There is a right time and a right place for everything. It all depends on local culture and custom. For example, in many parts of Nigeria, Burundi, Rwanda and Uganda the level of church commitment is so strong that it would be very strange for a visitor from a church-based AIDS programme not to offer a prayer at every visit. Indeed, if you do not offer to pray, it is very likely that you will be asked to do so. Prayer in the home is a usual, expected part of that community ministry. Prayer is a way of life. But in Thailand or parts of India the expectations may be very different. Spirituality is expressed in different ways. In countries like the UK, Ukraine or Russia, it is rarely expressed at all. And we need to be very sensitive to these things.

If you have developed a good caring and supportive relationship with someone over time, they will probably have sensed your beliefs, even though they may not share them. If they ask about your faith and hope, this is a wonderful opportunity to share a little of the hope that is in you, and perhaps to bring spiritual comfort and peace. They are driving the conversation, and it would be unfriendly not to answer their questions. You may find that in the context of their own searching, they find it reassuring to have someone around who has a faith. They may even ask you to pray for them. It is surprising how often a complete atheist has faith in the prayers of someone else! But in everything, your attitude must be that of a servant: how can I be of most help today? Also remember that you are always there as a guest and should only respond to questions, not initiate them.

What is important to you?

The first thing you may need to do is sort your own life out. I find it depressing to see how many people only really work out the meaning of their lives when their lives are almost at an end. Will it take a very serious medical diagnosis for you to put your own house in order? Urgent decisions may need to be made today to change your sex life or habit of injecting drugs, as well as to work out what is important to you.

What will really make you happy in the long term? Which are your most important relationships? I don't just mean this year, but over the next few years into the future. Do you know who your real friends are and to whom you belong?

These are important questions. Many people say after becoming a Christian: 'If only I had known then what I know now, my life would never have been such a mess.' The tragedy is that it often takes a serious medical event, or a near fatal accident, to make someone stop for long enough to think straight.

Living life to the full

You are important. I believe you were made for a purpose and that you will find your greatest happiness in discovering that purpose for yourself. Part of that involves starting to live for others. Jesus said that the only way you will find your true self – that is, become truly human – is by losing yourself; not by becoming a passive doormat that everyone else can tread on, but by letting go of the right to run your life your own way, and instead inviting Jesus to show you how to live life. I believe God has a plan for you and that because he loves you, his plan is the one that will make you truly happy.

The most important part of that plan is that he wants you to know him personally, as your friend, and that he wants you to have new power, strength and inner resources so that you can live life to the full. This brings wholeness and sometimes physical healing as well.

So then, we have looked at HIV prevention and care, seen many models that work, and seen how the church is being challenged to respond.

The next few chapters are about how to make a difference. They look at practical ways to make things happen in your own church and wider community, how to start a people movement to reach an entire community or nation, how to find resources for new HIV projects and how to make sure it is all sustainable and rooted in church life.

CHAPTER NINE

MAKING THINGS HAPPEN

This chapter explains how a small group of inspired Christian men and women can change their communities and help touch an entire nation.

What is God calling you to do?

There are all kinds of actions you can take that will be of practical help to those who have HIV. You might want to become a volunteer, to offer to visit someone who is ill, or to help support their family. Or you might want to help save lives by talking with people about how to protect themselves against HIV. Why not talk to others in your church, or to people who are already taking action in a Christian response to HIV, and offer your time to them.

Perhaps you are a church leader. You can start by talking about HIV in your leadership team, preaching about compassion, care and prevention, and by setting up a team to make sure practical steps are taken in your church and wider community.

But please don't stop there. You could help touch many thousands more lives. And here is how you could do it.

Always start with what you have

Remember how Jesus fed 5,000 with just five loaves of bread and two fish. I recently visited a school for AIDS orphans, funded by an income-generation project started by six grandmothers in a very poor area of Uganda. They prayed about their situation – they were looking after large numbers of grandchildren who were orphans, too poor to go to school. They felt God say that they should begin with what they had and get on with it themselves, gradually mobilising others in the village. Little by little the work has been established.

They saved up and bought some land. Then they saved to buy a cow. The milk from that cow pays to run the school. Gradually they made bricks and replaced the straw roof on poles with a small building. And then they built another. They started to teach the children as best they could in their own spare time. Everyone was helping. Some brought food, others cooked, and an old man carried water each day on his head, up from the valley, so the thirsty children could drink.

The grandmothers realised they needed some training and went off to government programmes to get a basic qualification. A visitor came and gave them money to get electricity. Another gave them a sewing-machine to train older girls. Another provided a pipe for running water.

'What will happen to the old man who brings water?' I asked, as carrying water for the school was his only income.

'He will sit under the tree and turn our tap, supplying all the rest of the village. Local people come to buy water from him, which helps him and helps our school.'

And gradually the work has grown.

Every church can encourage members to do something to help. As George Hoffman, the founder of Tearfund, once said: 'You can't change the whole world, but you can change someone's world somewhere.'

Go and change someone's life today. Go with food to a family stricken by HIV today. Go and comfort a widow or an orphan today. Go and find out how people living with HIV want to be helped. Go and encourage someone who is giving their lives to HIV ministry today. Pray for God's protection on them and for God's provision.

You may be part of the answer to those prayers! Find out how to give responsibly to projects that are making a difference in people's lives and support teams who are giving time and energy to help those affected by HIV. Use all the influence you have to encourage other people to take action today.

Learn from experience

Always learn from the experience of others. Life is too short to waste reinventing the same methods or materials. In January 2008, 170 people from 35 nations met in Uganda to look back on 20 years of HIV work, as part of the extended ACET family. We were joined by leaders from many international organisations such as Tearfund, Samaritan's Purse, Operation Mobilisation, the Salvation Army, PACANET and Scripture Union, as well as by leaders of many other projects.

What lessons could we learn? What are the best ways to start new work? What models work best? How can we run projects more effectively and with greater impact in future? What can we do to make funding easier? Here are some ideas that came from that meeting which you may be able to adapt to your own situation, whether you have a small project that is just beginning or a larger ongoing programme.

The importance of our faith was one key message that emerged. As teams we need to spend more time in prayer together, staying close to Jesus, who can give us all the wisdom and strength we need. It is really easy to lose focus because we are too busy in the work. It is also easy to lose our way chasing a dream, vision or ambition which is not God's plan for us. Many things are worth doing, but they may not be our own calling.

We need to keep in step with God, neither running ahead nor lagging behind. That is why we need other people around us, who can guide us, pick us up when we feel defeated, and pull us back when we are over-confident.

It is his work, not ours. We must always remember that.

Do research before taking big decisions

Listen, listen, listen before starting any new project. Do proper research into what the needs are and what others are already providing. If you think that you see a gap, talk some more with others in the community before trying to meet it. Also, talk early on to your church leaders. Do not rush into starting a new project.

If you are a church leader yourself, talk with other leaders you work with before starting a major project alone. David Kabiswa, Director of ACET Uganda, reminded me of a traditional saying: 'One who walks alone may go fast, but two who walk together go further.' If you can, join with others already doing the same thing. It is natural for a church to want their own programme but this can waste a lot of time, increase costs, restrict funding and prevent the 'light' from shining. Gather as many glowing coals as possible together on the fire to make the brightest light.

One very effective way for churches to have their 'own' work, while still enjoying being part of a wider national or international movement, is to work in a decentralised way. A regional centre can be based in a local church and 'owned' by them, while still sharing the same name as the national programme, accountable to a national board, registered as a national organisation. Because they share the same name as many programmes in other nations, they can still feel part of a global movement, able to join in bigger conversations with governments, international agencies and so on. This is how individual ACET projects work, linked as part of the ACET International Alliance.

Form a small team

If you are a church leader, one of the most important things is to set up a structure to take things forward. Appoint one of your most capable leaders to take responsibility for HIV activities in the church. One of their first tasks can be to form a small group to do some basic research into needs, and to help get some things started quickly.

Include the people you seek to help in your planning. Visit projects or churches in other areas with a similar model to the one you are proposing. If you cannot find another such project, start to worry. There are very few ideas that have not been tried before that will actually work, so if you are not heading for a Nobel prize for HIV prevention or care, think again. It may be there are really good reasons why no one else is doing similar work.

Start small but be ready with clear vision and plans to scale up fast. Do make sure that church leaders are backing what you are doing, or it could create trouble later. If your church leaders don't think your vision is right, take care. Do they think you are the wrong person to lead it, or is the project itself in need of a rethink? Is it an issue of timing, resources or direction? There may be a better way. Or maybe your leaders are just not interested in HIV.

If things get stuck you can always look to get involved in an existing organisation. You may even find there is no need for a new organisation after all.

When funds are available to pay staff, go first to your best volunteers. You know their commitment and quality, they have stood the test of time, and you know they are not just going to do the job for money.

Get organised

Remember to invest into organisation structure and capacity. More important than a separate office is a telephone line and answering machine, a mobile phone with SMS on a reliable network with good coverage, an email account (ideally two in case of problems) and at least two different places where you can get email access. Remember that book-keeping is vital to keep financial controls in order and to give accurate up-to-date information on what is being spent. Most new projects under-estimate just how much book-keeping time they will need.

Many of these things can easily be provided, at almost no extra cost, if the local project develops first under the umbrella of a local church, based in their offices. As the work grows, there may come a time when it is best to move out. Maybe the project is now so large that it is overwhelming the church office, or it needs to be in a more central location, which is not so closely identified with a particular church.

As you begin, be flexible and adapt to the situation as it unfolds. You will learn a huge amount in the first three to six months. Make yourself accountable right from the start to an independent board of supportive and friendly people you trust, who can encourage and advise you – and keep you from rushing into big mistakes. Be fast to admit mistakes and to learn from them. And keep praying – you need to have a daily sense of the presence of God, and to be filled with his power.

People who make things happen

Most new projects are started by what I call 'social entrepreneurs'. Organisations like Tearfund use terms like 'inspired individuals' to refer to these kinds of people. Entrepreneurs are people who love starting things, and they are pioneers, usually in business. Maybe you are one yourself.

They are exciting people to be with because they are full of ideas, full of vision, faith, energy and passion. They are great optimists and see huge opportunities around every corner. They also enjoy taking risks, and find total safety rather boring. They hate routine and doing the same things over again, and enjoy new situations. They thrive on change.

Social change-makers use their passion in changing the world. Sometimes they set up businesses to do this, with social agendas or to help generate income for existing projects, but more often they set up new projects and programmes to meet needs.

You often find these kinds of people are church planters and evangelists; people with strong faith and a personal sense of calling who are good at making things happen. They are great communicators, able to 'sell' new ideas in an attractive way, who engage the passions of others and push through barriers that most others would find too challenging. Other people are drawn to these social entrepreneurs, and want to work with them.

Strength of indigenous churches and role of women

In some parts of the world you will find more social entrepreneurs in locally instituted churches, rather than in denominations which have their roots in Europe or America. These indigenous churches often have far more members than older denominations, which may have more impressive buildings, many more committees and resources.

Older denominations may be more visible and appear to be more organised. However, they may sometimes be less flexible in thinking, less able to get new projects going. In contrast, locally instituted churches may be planting new congregations every few months, and may have much greater vision and energy when it comes to HIV.

Older denominations may have theology more similar to European churches. Local churches are more likely to place big emphasis on things like healing ministry, and to be lively and Pentecostal in style of worship and preaching.

Big international donors tend to think first about partnership with older, more familiar denominations, and find it much harder to relate to newer and less formal church groups. But they risk missing out on the most powerful church networks in the country.

Many social entrepreneurs in HIV work are women – for example, wives of senior pastors – especially in larger churches in places where women may otherwise have few opportunities to lead. They are often widely respected in local churches, able to mobilise huge numbers of other women to provide community care, schools prevention programmes and other things. In many nations women are starting large numbers of AIDS programmes, driven by huge compassion for those in need, and with huge talent for organisation.

Called to change the world

Social entrepreneurs can also be disturbing people to have around, and can sometimes create conflict – for example, on church leadership teams – especially if senior leaders do not like change and find it hard to cope with energetic people with loads of radical ideas. A great way to allow social entrepreneurs to channel their energy is for church leaders to encourage them to start new projects.

HIV projects are almost always started by social entrepreneurs. A few are started by managers or administrators, and these skills play a really important part in developing the work, but they rarely succeed unless they are driven by the energy and vision of a social entrepreneur who is closely involved and supporting them every day.

However, entrepreneurs often have a number of weaknesses. They may become impatient with people who slow things down; they might resist advice, are often over-confident and lack a wider perspective. They may be good at strong, rapid leadership decisions but poor in leading teams and delegating responsibility. Entrepreneurs often get bored rapidly and may have trouble completing complicated jobs. They are often tempted to leave projects too early, and find administration a burden. Entrepreneurs work best when they have others around them with strong management skills, who can pick up the project and take it into the implementation phase for the long haul.

Amazing things can happen when business entrepreneurs back social entrepreneurs with finance and practical advice. 'Venture philanthropy' is the term used when business people provide both funding and leadership on the board of an organisation, usually for a limited period – say, three to ten years. An example of this is the story of ACET UK, backed by World in Need. They provided not only three years of start-up funding, but also board members with huge experience (see pages 188–191).

Helpful tips for social entrepreneurs

- Decide if you *are* a social entrepreneur, and use your gifts if you are.
- Locate a key patron/mentor and personal guide.
- Focus on getting the details right. Do not wander off into new projects too soon. Do make sure that existing work is strong first.
- Deal with any tendency to boredom and attraction to new things, and stay focused with perseverance and self-discipline.
- Stay rooted in local church life – for protection of yourself, your family and your ministry.
- Ensure you have strong accountability/governance systems in place (see pages 188–191).
- Take time out regularly to reflect and pray, to stay on track.

Tips for encouraging social entrepreneurs

- Identify the next generation of social entrepreneurs. Listen to the visions of young people and encourage them with training and support.
- If you are a supporter or donor, accept a (small) risk of project failure in rapidly growing, entrepreneurial programmes.
- Bring social entrepreneurs together so they can support each other, but remember many by nature are quite competitive, which can make sharing more difficult.
- Help church leaders cope with social entrepreneurs who may sometimes be dismissed as a disruptive influence. They may be seen as unorthodox, too radical for the church, hard to manage, arrogant, self-opinionated and lacking in submission – and may be seen as a threat to the main mission of the church, by sucking resources away from projects which are higher priority.
- Give social entrepreneurs space to grow – release them from some of the structures of the church. Give them an independent board to help oversee them, but allow them freedom to develop work in new and creative ways.
- Do not suffocate social entrepreneurs with too many controls and committee meetings, but do pay careful attention to planning and financial management.
- If you are uncertain as a church leader, take the attitude of Gamaliel

to the disciples (Acts 5:38–39). If God is in the work, watch out! If not, it will probably fade away of its own accord. (However, this assumes that people are sensible with HIV projects and follow principles laid out in this and the next chapter).

- Pray that God will give you grace and wisdom. Living with social entrepreneurs is not easy!

So now we have looked at ways to make a difference and to start to make things happen, let us turn to people movements. How can we help create people movements to touch entire nations and beyond?

CHAPTER TEN

HOW PEOPLE MOVEMENTS CAN TOUCH NATIONS

Organisations, projects and programmes usually have limited impact compared to the potential impact of people movements, which can touch entire nations. We see this in history when men and women are inspired to act by a powerful vision which they take with them wherever they go, inspiring more people to do the same.

The early church was a people movement. It placed less emphasis than we do today on organisation and institutions, formal training programmes, seminaries and committee meetings. Its emphasis was more on faith, passion for a lost world, courage, determination and the power of the Holy Spirit.

As churches we are very good at creating new organisations that rapidly become rigid institutions with councils, rules and regulations. Before we know it, we have dampened the fire of new leaders and frustrated their passion. Of course we need strong organisations, and some of these should indeed become institutions, but there is another way. You can push the process below to the left (natural tendency) or to the right.

Institution ➤ organisation ➤ co-operation ➤ people movement

Sometimes we damage or destroy people movements by trying to control everything. We can stay as an institution, but moving to the right may mobilise far more people. The ACET movement only really began to accelerate when each programme became independent, self-governing, responsible to local boards, run (in almost every case) by local people.

Examples of recent people movements

I am sure you can think of people movements in your own country, but here are a few I know of personally, just from the UK.

March for Jesus

In 1987 in London, over 2,500 people walked in a procession while singing, worshipping and praying for the city. It was called 'March for Jesus'. By 1994 the idea of such marches had spread globally. On a single day over 10 million people marched in cities across 170 nations. By 2000 over 60 million marchers had taken part. It was all kept in motion by a small office team, who mailed out resources, produced a magazine, encouraged influential church leaders, spoke at conferences and so on.

Alpha

Alpha courses have now been attended by 11 million worldwide, with 33,500 courses in 163 nations. But it started as a small Bible study group in the 1970s in Holy Trinity Church, Brompton, London, before being redesigned by Nicky Gumbel in 1990. The idea of such a programme spread very fast across every denomination, fed by training conferences, a newspaper, books and other resources. A small team manages Alpha in Holy Trinity Church, but most of the work is done by volunteers all over the world, who use the training and resources.

24/7

In September 1999, a group of young people in England decided to pray non-stop for a month in relays, with different people turning up to a prayer room every hour. They then carried on until Christmas. Soon hundreds of temporary prayer rooms sprang up across the country and in other nations, usually just for a week at a time. As some rooms stopped, others started. This people movement became known as '24/7' – 24 hours a day, 7 days a week. The word spread from one person to another, through email and their website. Once again, 24/7 is supported by a very small team.

You get the picture. These people movements spread wider and faster than you might expect, as people seize the vision and make things happen, adapting to their own situation, carrying on the flame. They use training, events and well-produced resources to capture the imagination of millions.

The ACET people movement in Central Europe

Here is another example of a people movement, started by someone called Stuart Angus, who felt called to go to the Czech Republic in 1994. He had been trained as a schools educator by ACET UK, and had a vision for similar work in the Czech Republic. When he arrived, he wrote a book for young people about HIV and sexual health, and was able to do lessons in a few schools, but it was difficult to get invitations. After two years he decided to return to his own country, New Zealand.

Around 40 people came together to say goodbye and to pray. There were many tears. Tomas Rehak, an experienced Czech drugs worker, was deeply touched by God. It was as if someone in the UK had lit a candle in Stuart's heart and now he was lighting a candle in Tomas. Tomas knew he had to continue the work.

Within a few weeks, Tomas found many schools began to invite him. He quickly trained around 30 church volunteers, and a national programme was born, reaching around 60,000 young people a year. Most high school pupils in the Czech Republic now meet someone from the ACET team by the time they leave school. The programme continues to grow fast, in partnership with the Czech government and the European Union.

Milan Presburger was a youth worker in Slovakia when he heard about Tomas. He went to be trained, and then started a new ACET programme in Slovakia. He was asked by the government to train over 2,000 head teachers and 3,000 life-skills teachers. The Slovakia team reaches around 60 per cent of high school pupils.

Tomas then lit Marek Slansky's candle – a Czech student, supported by his own church as a worker in Siberia. Marek trained hundreds of Russian educators in over 90 cities, across 11 time zones, to help prevent the spread of HIV through sex and drug injecting. Since then, Tomas and other leaders have trained workers in eight other nations across the region.

Stuart 'accidentally' started a people movement all those years ago, with hardly any funding. What could God do through you in the future?

How to start a people movement – seven steps

People movements can touch the whole world. You cannot predict where one will start. Remember Jesus said that the Holy Spirit blows where he wills. But here are common patterns that we see before new people movements take off. In all you do, be prayerful and sensitive to what the Holy Spirit is doing, and keep Jesus central in everything. Act as if everything depends on you, and pray as if everything depends on God.

1. Tell your story

Make it personal – remember Moses and the burning bush. Moses had to tell his story before anything would happen. Your story really matters. Passion is infectious, powerful and can be dangerous to those who don't like change! Explain your calling and what you feel God has asked you to do and why.

2. Explain your mission – making a difference

People need to know what the need is, and how important and urgent it is. Moses gave clear explanations. Be very clear about how you aim, with God's help, to change the world. Have a short summary on printed sheets to give to people. If you are talking to a larger group, then PowerPoint and other presentation tools can really help – remember a picture is worth a thousand words and a 15-second inserted video clip is worth 10,000. Don't use more than a few words on a slide and keep slides moving quickly along as you tell your story. Watch a TV advertisement and see how many images flash by.

3. Reveal your strategy to key people

Jesus was careful who he told 'everything' to, and kept a lot for his disciples only. The full scale of your plans may scare some of your early supporters, so take care. They will understand more as they become involved. Try to involve the leaders of your church at an early stage. Their support is important. If they do not share the vision, you may need to carry on anyway, but keep praying and working at it.

4. Show the steps you have already taken – monitoring/evaluation

To win confidence from people who matter, show how you are already having an impact. Keep data, figures, letters of thanks, results. It is not enough simply to say you have seen amazing things happen.

5. Build credibility – support base, partnership

Look for key leaders or organisations that will lend their name to support you. They might be willing to be members of an advisory council, or to make a small donation so you can say your work is supported by them. The leaders of your church can help make this happen. Success tends to bring success. As Jesus said: 'To those who have, more will be given' (Matthew 25:29).

6. Make it easy for people to join you on the journey

Don't expect everyone in the church to share your passion and calling. We are all different parts of the same body of Christ – and each has different main areas of calling. But do make it easy for people to make some kind of response, however limited. For example, I often encourage people to take a free copy of this book – on condition they give it away to a leader or project worker in a high-incidence country. It is a small thing that almost anyone can do and helps them feel involved.

7. Equip, release and empower other leaders

The final test of mature leadership is to do what Jesus did: give it away. Don't try to control everything. When you give leadership to others, stay involved and supportive, or people may think your passion has gone, and maybe theirs will too. Remember the 'founder syndrome' – many organisations start to slow down and some fail to survive because an energetic, visionary founder has been unable to hand things on to someone who can take things to a new level. So expect new leadership to do things differently from you. Trust God that it is his work and that he will take care of it all. Be supportive and encouraging.

How to grow large programmes with small teams

Large national programmes can grow rapidly more easily with small national offices if leadership is decentralised – as ACET has seen in places like Russia, Ukraine and Slovakia. It is impossible to create a people movement with a lot of central control – you will just create a strong traditional organisation.

To decentralise well means developing a 'contract' or formal agreement between the national leader and each regional team leader – in a similar way to how you would with a large donor. This agreement should contain:

- Clear areas/regions of responsibility.
- Plans for local action for the next 12 months.
- Outline of work patterns.
- Limits for decision making.
- Regularity of meetings to assess progress, for support and guidance.
- Details of how they will measure/monitor what they do.
- Funding costs for each month or quarter.
- Details of how funds will be transferred from national to regional teams.
- Details of record-keeping on a monthly basis.
- Notes on what will happen if they are over-spent or under-spent on budget.
- How reports will be generated, by what date and by whom.
- What will happen if there is a disagreement – who else gets involved.
- An outline of how what they do fits into the national programme.
- What input they will have into decisions about national and regional issues.

The national leader then becomes the leader of several relatively self-contained regional groups. He or she is responsible for vision, overall management and quality control; overall strategy; new programmes not under regional structures (yet); training and support of regional leaders; running the national team (including regional leaders – values, ethos, common issues, strategy formation); reporting to international and national donors; fund-raising – with help from regional leaders in generating applications/reports.

Work through the local church

In practice, as things decentralise, you may find that each regional team already has a very close relationship with a particular church – probably the church that the regional team leader belongs to.

The leaders of that church may be able to help provide stability, oversight, support, training, encouragement and some financial control for the regional team. In Russia, for example, over 300 ACET educators work in more than 90 cities, based around 90 churches. These church leaders can play a vital part in developing future plans and vision, as part of the mission of their own church.

Some people worry that if a team has grown out of a local church, other churches or denominations may not want to be involved. But it all depends on local relationships with other leaders who can be involved at an early stage. You can also vary things so that training programmes are hosted by different churches. You can make sure that team members are from more than one church, or appoint members of different churches as board members.

If you are a national organisation, you can base local offices in, say, a Baptist church, another in a Pentecostal church, another in an African-instituted (indigenous) church and another in an Anglican church and so on.

The truth is that I would much rather base a new work in a large church with strong vision, with full backing of the leaders, than be based in a small office in town, with no commitment by any church leaders from any church.

But every situation is different. You may know the work will grow quickly, with good support from different leaders, and that you need to find a base outside of any church for various reasons. Maybe your government would not accept you as a professional partner if you were seen to be too closely linked to a church, for example.

In some countries it is not even possible to register a Christian health organisation, and if church links appear too strong, an HIV project can be closed down immediately – workers could even land up in prison. You need to be very wise, and get expert advice in such situations to make sure you are always operating within the law. In some places it may be that the only way you can operate is to register as a secular organisation providing HIV care and prevention.

Recruit the right people

Take special care with recruitment. Before you offer a job, make sure you are clear about what the need really is, and the skills required. Draw up a detailed job description. What kind of person are you praying for? Consider how you can assess them during an interview, what questions to ask, what areas to explore concerning their motivation. Setting a task or short presentation as part of the interview can be very revealing.

When appointing, make sure at least two other people are involved in making the decision. It is easy to make mistakes, and this person needs to fit into the existing team. Talk to people they have worked with in the past and maybe their church leaders. If it is a very important role, consider appointing them first on probation, on a trial basis, to see how things work out.

Your best volunteers are often great people to employ: you know they are committed to you and passionate about the cause. They understand the work. You have been able to see them in action. They are already trained. They are part of the team. It is less likely that they are just motivated by money. If funding becomes a problem, they are more likely to work once more as volunteers rather than leave the organisation.

Be true to your values

If you want to build a strong programme, be clear about your core values: these are the principles that underlie everything. They affect *how* you operate rather than the detail of what you *do*. They are like your genetic code. They describe the Christian spirit in which you work, your culture and the nature of your 'family'.

What are your values?

Some ACET leaders met recently and produced a list of values that their programmes share in common with many other faith-based organisations. They are aims; things they try to live up to.

- Showing God's love to the world – especially to those who may feel least valued in their societies.
- Empowering people to take action to help themselves and others.
- Inspiring men and women to make a difference.
- Placing a high value on relationships, team working, co-operating, partnership, a sense of family for all those connected with the programme – whether staff, volunteers or those receiving help.
- Church mobilisation: working closely with churches at every level.
- Excellence and effectiveness: being highly professional in everything.
- Evidence-informed: using results of research/evaluation to shape and improve programmes.

- Community-based: emphasis on working within, or in partnership with, existing structures, organisations, activities, homes, churches – rather than constructing huge and expensive buildings and running things separately.
- Prophetic: seeking to live out a message of compassion and hope in a way that challenges society.
- Focusing on youth – not only because they are often most at risk, but because they are often able to give most time.
- Strong management systems – able to take some risks to achieve high impact.
- Using community networks and organisations.
- Involving community in planning and decision-making.
- Using technology to reduce costs, improve communication, work fast and increase impact.
- Being sensitive to local culture, listening carefully and adapting as necessary.
- Flexibility: situations change and new needs or opportunities emerge.
- Being creative and innovative – thinking about new ways to do things, learning.
- Networking with other organisations to do things more easily.
- Developing partnerships with both faith and non-faith groups – not trying to do it all ourselves (costs too much and too slow).
- Working across as many denominations as possible – uniting the body of Christ in a single purpose.
- Staying true to biblical values, the foundation of church life for 2,000 years.
- Strengthening local churches, organisations and communities, rather than competing with them.
- Choosing programme leaders of the same nationality and culture as those they seek to reach –possible in almost all situations.

So then, we have looked at how to double the impact of our work or ministry, and how to help create a people movement of men and women stirred up to make a difference, to help save lives, prevent spread of HIV and care for those affected.

People movements are usually driven by large informal groups of volunteers. But what do we mean by 'volunteer', and how should they be recruited and managed?

CHAPTER ELEVEN

GROWING TEAMS OF VOLUNTEERS

Volunteering is a central part of the Christian tradition as people follow the call of Jesus to lay down their lives for others in need. Without volunteers, most churches would cease to function.

Most ACET programmes benefit from time given by volunteers – either free of charge or for far less than the commercial rate. But what exactly do we mean by volunteers? As you look around the world you will see some who are:

- paid by other organisations – e.g. schools educators who are supported by their churches;
- making a gift of their time without the expectation of any financial help, except maybe with travel expenses;
- happy to give a lot of time, but expect some small stipend to assist them with basic living.

Volunteer case study: ACET Ukraine

ACET Ukraine has been really successful in attracting, training and keeping over 400 volunteer schools workers in just over four years. Here are steps any project can follow:

- Explain the vision, need and opportunity clearly.
- Show how each volunteer can make a real difference.
- Use attractive materials to promote the work.
- Use existing volunteers to recruit their friends.
- Talk to pastors about promoting the programme in their church.
- Train people who are sent from partner organisations, church youth workers, etc.

- Make programmes easy to join and high quality, to get a good reputation.
- Give volunteers tasks they can do easily and confidently.
- Give them lots of support and encouragement.
- Keep training as short as possible – respect their time.
- Have formal presentations, with certificates, at the end of training.
- Phone every new volunteer two weeks after training to ask:
  - Did you enjoy it?
  - Are you still keen to help us?
  - Can we get you started soon?
  - Can we book some dates right now?
- Phone every volunteer once a month, without fail, to ask:
  - How are you?
  - How are you getting on?
  - What sort of bookings do you have for the future?
- Ask each volunteer to send you the reports and evaluation forms each month. (Some national teams give small rewards to those who send in their reports.) Give each volunteer encouraging news on a regular basis, to help them feel part of the family.
- Bring all volunteers together each year to:
  - Share news and celebrate success.
  - Show new materials/ideas/lesson plans.
  - Introduce volunteers who have joined the staff team.
  - Hear encouraging stories from different regions.

Stipends? Living by faith?

Using volunteers can raise complex issues of justice, minimum wage and so on. In South Africa and some other nations it is expected (or even required by government) that volunteers receive a small stipend. It may be a small financial gift or food parcels or other support, in addition to help with travel costs.

Another issue is that governments may pay a project to provide a basic government service – for example, counselling and HIV testing. Maybe they are doing so to save money. Maybe the reason why your service is cheaper than their health service is because church members are giving their time (almost) for nothing. Should the government not pay your team properly for work you are doing for them? But are you then just propping up the state healthcare system with people who are being paid far less than the 'correct' rate for the job?

Also, if someone is 'living by faith', depending on God's daily provision rather than on a formal salary, is that person a volunteer or not? What happens when such a 'volunteer' who is 'living by faith' ends up securing more personal income from friends and people in the church than salaried full-time staff?

These things need to be talked about in management teams.

The real cost of volunteers

When we rely on volunteers, it can hide the real costs of running a programme. Just because people give their time, we should not value them any less than if we were paying their salaries. We should take just as much care to make sure their time is used well, taking into account their skills and experience. Too often I see very well-qualified and capable volunteers 'helping out' with basic tasks that many less able people could easily do.

Volunteers may cheerfully do all kinds of things for us, but it may not be the best stewardship of resources. Of course in a small organisation everyone has to do all kinds of basic tasks from time to time, and we do so with humility, as servants. But do not misuse eager volunteers just because they are happy to do anything. Think every day about how to use them more strategically.

Having said that, it can often be hard to get a perfect match between skills and tasks. I remember a retired doctor once offering himself to an ACET home-care team in London. The trouble was that we did not really have enough extra medical work for him to do in all the time he had available. So we created extra research roles and other activities he could help with.

The value of 'gifts of time' can be shown in the accounts: 'Our programme costs were £10,000 last year, but that did not take into account around £15,000 of volunteer time – if they had been paid for the time they gave.' Or: 'The income of our programme was £10,000 last year, not including gifts of more than £15,000 – the value of time given by volunteers.'

Volunteers can be hard to manage. They can come and go without commitment. It can be hard to make demands on them, because they are giving their time. It is vital to have a formal agreement with key volunteers you really depend on – so you and they are clear about what is expected. Without clarity, you will find it very hard to use volunteers in positions of real responsibility.

Volunteers from other nations – or local leadership?

Here is a very sensitive issue. What about volunteers who arrive from other countries, like America, the UK and Australia, to work in some of the poorest parts of the world? These foreigners may bring vitally needed skills, vision and experience. Without them, it may be that many projects would not have started in the past, or would have grown more slowly. But there are questions we must ask.

At first sight these volunteers may appear to be cost free, but they are not. The fact is that their churches and friends back home have probably been asked to provide a huge sum in air fares and support costs, compared to the costs of local salaries in the places they are working. Or they may be covering their own costs from their own savings. But if that same amount were to be donated as a general gift to the project they are helping, the project leaders would probably be shocked. Return air fares alone for a family could cost over $16,000. Then you have to add whatever else they will need – house rent, costs of education, food, vehicle, fuel, phone, taxes, security and so on.

In the poorest parts of the world, $300 a month can be a significant salary, and $150 a month may be enough to help support a project worker part time. Local costs vary a lot of course, but one thing is clear. It is almost always far cheaper and better for the community to employ local people from the country where the project is based, rather than buying in people from wealthy nations.

Here is a test: if a church decided to give a local project in a place like Zambia the choice between employing 10 to 20 local people or having one 'volunteer' from the UK, which would they choose? You will soon find out if you send the money into the project bank account and let them make free choices, in the light of all the demands on their budget. Let them pay the air fares and school fees, the rent and the vehicle costs – or maybe they will decide to employ loads of local people after all.

Short-term international visits – yes or no?

It is the same with short-term trips where people pay maybe $2,000 each (air fares, etc.) to help build an orphanage for two weeks. It can be an appalling misuse of resources, unless there is a more important reason for going. For a start, they are probably taking work away from local labourers who may be earning only $3 a day.

Short trips to other nations are vitally important: not usually to give time, but rather to learn. People then return deeply touched and fired up as ambassadors and fund-raisers for the project for the rest of their lives. Or they may need to visit to monitor progress of projects that are already receiving significant support.

But please don't pretend your short visit is a valuable gift of time, unless there really is a specific need maybe for the training and skills that you have, which the project is asking for, and really cannot be met by directing them to other local people. Project leaders may be too polite to tell you the truth; too polite to decline your kind offer. They may believe that it is good for you to come in the hope that more sponsorship may follow after you return.

Sadly many people in the church in places like Europe or America will give generously to a friend or family 'going out to serve God', or even to fund a student to build an orphanage for two weeks. But the same people are often far less likely to be as generous in funding the salaries of local believers in that same project – even though they may be vastly cheaper and better qualified in language, culture, skills and local acceptability.

I have seen HIV programmes in the poorest parts of the world which are swamped with European or American workers. The same projects struggle to fund local salaries! How absurd – a scandal in fact. It is easy to talk all the right words about sustainable development. It is easy to talk about building capacity and empowering local people. But it is also easy to end up robbing local people of jobs and leadership at the same time.

Of course such people from other nations often have important roles to play, but the best balance is usually for someone to visit, do some training and then return, with little risk of undermining project leadership. It is really important for expatriates to look for every opportunity to hand over to nationals. Sometimes local leadership will only rise up when the expatriate is forced to leave by the government.

The world is changing – new models of partnership

These are very difficult issues. In the past two centuries, entire mission-ary organisations existed to send people from one nation to another, as messengers of the gospel, often into great dangers, and many lost their lives, mainly dying rapidly of disease. These brave men and women made the ultimate sacrifice for Christ and the fruit of their labour is seen all over the developing world today – hospitals they built, schools they established, theological colleges they started – and in the generation of national church leaders they trained.

More recently, two out of 20 ACET programmes would never have started without a national from a wealthier nation moving to a poorer nation, making the country their own, devoting their entire lives to supporting churches in saving lives and caring for the sick.

But I am challenging us all to see the new direction of mission in the third millennium, where the situation is changing rapidly and where churches in these nations are now often healthier and stronger than those of the traditional 'sending' nations. Decades of education have created generations of highly skilled Christian workers, and these 'receiving' nations are now sending missionaries back to secularised countries like the UK.

Regular visits to projects from wealthier nations

People from other nations or cultures can also get into difficulties as regular visitors, rather than residents in a country. They are usually seen as far wealthier, more influential, and with access to donors. All of this is true. Anyone who owns their own car is a multimillionaire com-pared to most people in the world. Project leaders may defer to visitors too often, and be afraid to say when their visitors are becoming too influential or are visiting too often.

Remember that regular project visits can be very disruptive – meeting people at airports, giving hospitality, looking after them from dawn to night, driving them everywhere (even to do shopping or get money from a bank), taking them on site visits, meeting the team. Normal project work may stop altogether for days at a time. Five to ten project visits a year by different people can bring a programme to a halt.

Each person or group may be totally unaware of other visits the previous or following week. Project leaders may not tell them because they want them to feel really special, as part of being hospitable. It is also possible that they would prefer them not to know too much about who else they get support from.

I have often had to help visitors from wealthy nations with strong emotional ties to projects to let go and step back to allow space for national leadership. Often they feel they have to keep on returning to do more training or capacity building, even when programmes are clearly developing their own skills, or have access to similar or better training in their own nations, from people with the same language and culture, at a fraction of the cost. Are they really serving the project, or is the project now serving their need to be needed? These issues can be very painful and take a long time to work through.

Foreign visitors may say: 'But my methods of training are better than those from other organisations in the country.' Are we really certain? We may feel we bring a special spiritual dimension. Maybe, but it is often the other way round. Their spirituality may outshine that of visitors from more materialistic cultures.

Finally, visitors from other nations may say: 'But I am going out of relationship, a close sense of connection, friendship, to encourage the team and support them.' That is great! All I am saying is we should think first. We should pray and reflect carefully before jumping on planes – even if the invitation is warm and sincere – and we should make every day count. We may be able to achieve almost all we think is needed in half the time.

I am not saying people should stop visiting. By all means they should visit, stay a while even, but they should just be sensitive – and careful.

So then, we have seen how new projects can grow quickly as people use the time, energy and resources they already have, create teams, motivate others, and are well organised.

We have seen how social entrepreneurs can inspire large numbers of people to give time and money. We have seen how small decentralised teams based in churches can help touch an entire nation. We have seen how good models can multiply, spreading as a people movement around the world. We have also seen how vital it is to stay true to our faith, calling and values.

But there is a problem. Many HIV projects start off well and then get stuck. They find that they cannot grow. They may lack staff with the right skills, or lack funding. They cannot find a way forward. The next chapter gives us some answers as it explores how to build strong, effective HIV programmes.

CHAPTER TWELVE

HOW TO BE TWICE AS EFFECTIVE

Many Christian projects are inefficient and wasteful. They take far too long to make simple decisions. They keep going back over old decisions instead of getting on with the job. They waste time by not sharing out tasks within a team. They spend too many hours in long meetings. People waste time repeating work others have already done in the project, or duplicating efforts by workers in another project, or travelling back and forth because they did not plan ahead. Many leaders waste effort doing things they find hard, instead of asking for help. They work in isolation instead of co-operating with others and sharing resources.

It is often easy to improve this dramatically at relatively low cost. Just look at the time saved with a single SMS (text message) to warn several people you are late because an accident forced your vehicle into a ditch, and then being able to contact a garage. But did you have their phone numbers with you? Did you remember to charge up your phone? Did you have enough credit on your phone card?

David Kabiswa, head of ACET Uganda, often reminds me: 'Strong organisations mean strong projects.' Many HIV projects reach a certain level and find it hard to grow further. They lack resources and can get discouraged and tired.

In this chapter are keys for any project to be stronger, more effective, more sustainable. These keys can be used in any organisation – not just ones related to HIV.

But before we start, here is a question. Are you sure God is calling you to be a larger organisation? Take care here. It is easy to be carried along by a great vision which may not actually be God's calling on you. If you have a home-care team in your church with 30 volunteers, are you sure you are called to grow it to 100? If you are reaching 10,000 students a year, are you sure you are called to reach 100,000? It may be that other groups or churches will develop into those things.

However, one thing is clear. Whether our project is large or small, we have a moral duty to make sure we have the maximum impact with the resources we have. So how can we run projects more effectively? How can we be more efficient, do work of higher quality, have greater impact, save more lives, reach more people, and succeed in finding more resources? How can we make sure that funding continues for the work and increase support? How can we find and develop leaders? How do we make sure we stay true to God's calling?

Shorter, better meetings – and how to double productivity

Plan, plan, plan. Organise, organise, organise. When you meet, be clear about your main purpose. Agree the list of things you will discuss, decisions you need to make today, and in what order. Keep to time, make sure each voice is heard, make notes of decisions and make sure each person who attends gets their own copy as soon as possible after the meeting. Make sure people keep to their promises. Be very clear about what needs to be done and by when. Give people key tasks. Check that they really understand exactly what is needed. Check they have all they need to do it. Check up regularly on progress – and review all action points at your next meeting.

Email is the most efficient way to communicate longer messages with people in larger organisations around the world. Check email regularly to keep things moving. Put email access, mobile phones and computing into your budgets.

Remember that *work always expands to fill the time available.* If you have three weeks to do a report, it will take three-and-a-half weeks. If you have only three days, it will take you less than a week. Be ruthless about your use of time. When you ask people to do things, give deadlines, and do not let the task run on too long.

The 80:20 rule

Remember the 80:20 rule of management. In most things in life, around 80 per cent of the impact comes from 20 per cent of the effort. Almost all your volunteers may come from just 1 in 5 of the churches you work with. Around 80 per cent of your income may come from only 20 per cent of donors; 80 per cent of schools visits may be done by 20 per cent of your volunteers; 80 per cent of your people with HIV at home may live in 20 per cent of the villages. Most of your impact as a leader may come from just a few hours a week of your time. It is just a way to think about focusing on what is really important. The actual numbers may vary, of course.

So what is your 80:20? What do you do in a day or a week which has more impact than anything else you do?

Jesus applied a similar principle and was very focused: he sent out 120 on a mission but focused on 12 disciples. Of the 12, he spent most time with three – Peter, James and John. Of his earthly life of 33 years (15 as an adult), he spent just three in public teaching.

Cut out some of the things you do which have small impact but take significant time – or delegate them to others. Your life as a leader is far too short to do things that other people are willing and able to do – even if they do not do them quite as well as you would do them yourself.

Make every hour of every day count. What can I do in the next half an hour that could have more impact on the work than anything else I can do in the whole week? What call should I make now? What email should I write next? What report should I force myself to complete? What meeting should I arrange? What team member should I spend time with? Pray constantly about these things.

A key way to maximise impact is to do what Jesus did: disciple key workers who can take on major responsibilities. It could be the most effective use of two to three hours a week. But are you doing it?

You will be amazed at what can happen when you and your team are more focused.

Sort out your priorities

Every organisation needs to be clear about its priorities so that energy is focused where it really matters. The global leadership of the ACET family met recently. Here are the priorities they came up with – as examples. Yours might be very different.

- Assist the growth and maturity of existing and new national programmes.
- Develop high quality resources that can be used widely.

- Strengthen regional teams for the support and capacity building of projects.
- Ensure rapid development of clinical care in collaboration with national authorities to fill key gaps at their request, such as: voluntary testing and counselling, provision and supervision of antivirals, focusing particularly on pregnant women shortly before birth.
- Give special focus to Southern African nations where the HIV problem is now greatest.
- Develop joint funding bids on a regional basis to international donors/government agencies, using specialists in key countries such as Ireland and the UK.
- Develop joint advocacy campaigns on key issues across regions and beyond. Micah Network and the Ecumenical Advocacy Alliance are examples of faith-based agencies with international advocacy roles (www.e-alliance.ch and www.micahchallenge.org/).

HIV project planning cycles

Using clear planning cycles is vital to meet donors' expectations and to provide good leadership:

Vision to plan to execution to evaluation – then back to vision . . .

The minimum length for project planning is usually three years, with annual reviews, unless working to a time-limited event such as organising a conference. A common process of planning is called 'Project Cycle Management'. It takes time to build a team, develop a programme, speed up progress and improve processes as you go. You need to evaluate at the end of the first year to decide if major changes need to be made during the second year.

Management by objectives

Evaluate your work as objectively as you can, using indicators agreed at the start.

Management by Objectives (MBO) was invented by Peter Drucker over 50 years ago. He said: 'If something is not measured, it is unlikely to happen.'

For each group of objectives there may be a key performance

indicator: one piece of information that is vital in understanding what is happening. For a homecare team in India, for example, it could be the number of new clients seen each month (which tells them about workload, demand for the service and so on). For a schools programme it could be number of pupils seen per month, number of classes taken and number of schools visited.

Many international development agencies love this approach and like to see clear lists of objectives and, against each one, actions to be taken, how you will know you have succeeded, what the risks are, how you will reduce risks and so on.

This planning is often called a 'log frame', or a 'logical framework', and it is now required by many donors. Completing one is a discipline because it makes you think hard about what you are planning to do. It can also be an excellent way for you to assess progress against your own targets. Log frames can be used by donors to make rapid comparisons between projects.

However, many project leaders hate log frames. If they become too complicated, they may not help in actually managing things from day to day. They are certainly time-consuming to complete, and can limit programme thinking to key variables/measures. So try to keep it all as simple as you can.

Holistic mission can be damaged, partly because many of the most important outputs can be hardest to measure – such as the long-term impact of training 100 leaders across the country. But log frames are here to stay. Make sure donors understand they need to fund not only your project, but also the important time preparing log frames, writing reports and doing evaluations.

ROOTS 5 on Project Cycle Management from Tearfund is an excellent introduction to log frame planning. *http://tilz.tearfund.org/ Publications/ROOTS/Project+cycle+management.htm*

Show how you make a difference

There are many shining examples of outstanding Christian HIV projects. However, for too long many donors and governments have associated Christian programmes with well-meaning people muddling along, doing their best but lacking professionalism. We need to raise standards in every area, whether in care and prevention, record-keeping, financial control, staff training or anything else.

We need to show that our programmes are effective – using methods recommended by international experts. God has given us time, energy and other resources, and we are responsible for using them wisely. That means thinking about what we do, and how to do it better.

Monitoring means evaluating what the team is doing. Collecting useful data will show you what is working best and how to improve. You can also show your supporters what you are doing, win the support of church leaders, and the favour of governments. You can show donors the value of your work and how cost-effective you are, in a way they will understand.

Donors have to prove the impact of the money they give, so we need to help them. Many large donors are fascinated by the power of churches to mobilise communities. They know that the majority of 'faith-based' projects in many nations are Christian. But others are cautious, and your programmes will need to show their strength clearly.

There is a shortage of well-run projects with well-written reports showing they are doing good work. If you are one of these, you are already a big step closer to finding new financial support. But it is not enough to tell stories. You need data, graphs, tables, maps, diagrams, photographs. And lots of them. One good quality and interesting picture, table, graph or map can be worth a thousand words. Use short, focused, fast-moving slide presentations with donors and important visitors.

Help donors with clear proposals that explain the urgent need, what you are doing and why what you are doing is so vital and unique in the situation. Explain how your work fits in with what other agencies are doing, use data to show size and impact, and provide a detailed budget. Keep reports to just a few pages.

Some examples of data that a project could collect

- Surveys which give evidence that student attitudes have changed after your presentations.
- Number of home visits to those with HIV, and length of each visit.
- Number of new people with HIV referred to your clinic each month: age, gender, ethnic group and why they have come.
- School lessons given each month; number of different schools and total attendance; number of new schools educators trained and number becoming inactive, and how many active educators.

- Number of training programmes for church leaders and community leaders, and numbers attending.
- Numbers and types of people or groups reached by each person in the first year after training.
- Number of orphans receiving food support/help with school fees each month.
- Radio/TV broadcasts and estimated total audience – the broadcaster will know what estimates are for each hour of the day.
- DVDs/books/magazines distributed to project workers.
- Number of people given counselling and voluntary testing for HIV.
- Percentage of positive tests.
- Number of pregnant women identified each month, number successfully transferred to the local hospital for care and free antiviral treatment.
- Number on antiviral treatment visited each week to encourage correct use of medication.

And so on. Make sure you agree with donors what statistics they want to see at the end of the year, that what they are asking is reasonable, and that costs of monitoring and evaluation are included in the proposal.

Almost every activity you do can be measured in numbers in some way. However, many really important things can be hard to measure, such as how peaceful and comfortable a dying person feels. Yes, you could do a survey, but it would not be appropriate.

There is often debate about what data is best to prove impact – or if it can be proved at all. Remember, the most important reason for collecting these numbers is not for your donors, but to help you see quickly what is going on, so you can manage a changing situation.

One picture or graph can be worth a thousand words

Every well-run project should have a simple report on a single sheet or two of paper which is often updated, showing you not only what the figures are compared to what you were expecting, but also how they have changed. Make sure the indicators are clear, reliable and up to date. Simple graphs are much more helpful than lists of figures. For example, you could have one showing the number of schools visited each month, but remember to add to the graph in other colours the same data for previous years, so you can compare the seasonal ups and downs. A graph will show you in less than two seconds if you have a major problem.

Look for key indicators – ones which tell you more information at a glance than all the others. For example, I get sent monthly newsletters by the Nireekshana ACET HIV clinic in Hyderabad. It is full of photos, stories and news. But I always turn to the back page, which has some data on the previous month. Out of all the figures, there is one simple number that tells me if the care work is healthy or in crisis, if the team are encouraged or depressed, whether they are coping or overwhelmed.

It is the number of new patients seen – usually around 65. If the number were to fall to 30 for two months I would know the team would be wondering what was happening, if the needs of people with HIV were being better met elsewhere, if the epidemic was slowing down, if something had gone wrong with the quality of the project, if they needed to advertise the service more widely. If the numbers jumped to over 100 I know they would be feeling stretched, wondering if they will increase further soon – in which case they would urgently need more staff, and so on.

Manage risks to help prevent disasters

Many Christian organisations sleepwalk into danger, not really thinking too much about the future, trusting that somehow God will sort it all out. We must plan ahead and manage risks in both small things and major things.

2 Thessalonians 3:10 says: 'He who does not work, does not eat.' This could also mean: 'He who does not manage risks, does not have a project any longer' – managing risk is just a form of work after all.

How can you minimise potential risks without spending too much time and effort? Many projects close because they failed to manage risks.

The first thing is to make a list. Then against each item you and your team can begin to think about ways to reduce that risk. The amount of effort you make on risk reduction will depend on how serious the risk is: what is the likelihood of this thing happening? What is the possible impact? For example, your project leader is unlikely to be suddenly knocked out by serious illness or an accident, but if the project would collapse as a result of this happening, you need to plan now how you would manage. Your computer could easily be stolen, which would cost a lot to replace, and mean you lose valuable data. Think about insurance, and backing up your data each day.

Your risks could include things like:

- Poorly trained volunteer who damages the project's reputation.
- Major accident on the road.
- Applying too late for a visa – very common!
- Someone stealing from the project.
- Late arrival of large donations.
- Not being able to pay rent or salaries because of poor planning and lack of discipline in keeping to a budget.
- Forgetting to allow for price increases where inflation is high.
- Relying on one person to do everything – who then becomes sick or has to leave the country.

Risk example: loss of data could destroy your project

A common crisis in a project is caused by a major loss of computer data. All computers break down – even new ones. The causes may be mechanical, software problems or virus attack. Unless you act now, one day you will probably lose all your files, emails and financial records. Portable computers fail even more often. Computers are also easily stolen – along with all your back-up disks, tapes, CDs and USB sticks.

It may be impossible to recover from this kind of loss if no copies have been kept. Just rebuilding an address book of volunteers and supporters can take weeks. People have lost entire drafts of books, years of Bible notes, a decade of valuable project photos, entire training programmes, months of accounts, vital donor records and reports. Months of time spent recovering is time that should have been spent training people, caring for those who are sick, planning new projects or talking to donors. Project output and income falls, and costs rise. Data loss can be serious enough to destroy a project and cause it to close.

I am astonished and dismayed at how few people take responsibility for backing up their own data every day or few days. Data back-up MUST be a number one priority for every professional project that uses computers.

Get two large external disk drives and routinely back up all changes every day or couple of days. Use different disk drives each week and take the second one to a different location altogether (not in the office). Hide the one that is in the office very carefully – or a thief could steal both computers and back-up.

Set a formal routine. Use a wall chart to show when back-ups were last done and by whom. Use a small USB stick for your own really important files as extra security. Take special care with email. Programs like Outlook can be hard to back up – search on Google for instructions.

So then, we have looked at ways to get things done, to help start people movements, to use volunteers and to be more effective as leaders. We now need to turn to another big stumbling-block for many great HIV projects: lack of capacity.

CHAPTER THIRTEEN

BUILDING EXTRA PROJECT CAPACITY

Why building capacity could be the most important thing we do

Many Christian organisations have very limited *capacity* to grow or get things done. Everyone seems to be under huge work pressures. There are many demands.

You may be short of people with the right skills. Workers may need extra training. Leaders may lack planning skills. They may find it hard to create financial budgets or to list the steps they need to take. The ability to plan ahead and work out *all* the steps from A to B is a really important skill. They may be short of funds, and unsure of how to attract donors, or to raise money from church members.

We need to do what Jesus and the early church did: invest time in a small number of key people, who in turn will be able to train and lead others. You may find it easier to build capacity if your roots are deep within a church, so you are not just seen by your leaders as someone doing things on their own, unconnected with the mission of the church in any way. If your own church owns the vision, then many things can happen fast. You may be allowed to use space in the church as an office, and share resources such as phone lines, internet, computers and photocopiers.

Church leaders may promote the work among the congregation, provide financial help, encourage other churches to get involved and open doors to speak at national church conferences. They may provide experienced senior leaders as board members or advisors. You may find many of your most committed volunteers come from that church.

Things often work best if one 'main' church helps set up a new HIV programme as an independent legal organisation, but with church

Build capacity

Capacity is a combination of factors, such as leadership capability, ways of organising, cultural norms and physical assets such as buildings. As we have seen many times in Uganda, these things can either help organisations respond effectively – or hold them back.

The church needs to keep central the compassion of Christ, and to recognise what it does best. For example, your church may have a long history of sending youth workers into schools. Adding HIV lessons to what they do is easy. Building capacity means working out what the real needs are and how best to help. It also means measuring the difference you make, and learning both from mistakes and from what goes well.

One way to increase capacity is to start new HIV programmes. Or you can expand existing HIV projects, or add HIV activities into other programmes. In all three cases, careful management of your limited resources is really important: people, buildings, time, funding. Look to work in partnership with others, especially networks of people living with HIV.

Sometimes more resources are available than a church or project is able to use properly or quickly enough. For example, a donor may be willing to provide a large grant, but only if the work can double in size in a year. When there are limits to capacity – maybe in leadership, or people with the right skills – opportunities are easily lost. Funding can quickly disappear. People move on to other things. Buildings fill up with less important activities.

Capacity-building aims to help leaders develop programmes that can grow safely, rapidly and on strong foundations, in a way that can be sustained for a long time.

A key way to create more capacity is to go and visit other, stronger organisations which do similar work, and learn from how they operate. Recruit people with skills you do not have, who you think are more talented, gifted and faith-filled than you are. It is a real test of courage, but is a powerful way to grow. Share your needs with the leaders of your church.

Paul Kabunga, Head of ACET Africa Region and Deputy Director, ACET Uganda

leaders/members on the board. They continue to feel pride and ownership in a special way.

As the work grows, broaden representation on your board to keep the right balance of skills and background. Make sure the project director is happy about each appointment.

Lessons for capacity-builders

- **Develop a clear 'contract'** with those you are partnering if you are aiming to build capacity in another organisation. Be clear on objectives, method and timescale, what they want. Agree what help you are able to give and what is expected of them.
- **Be disciplined** in the use of time, and be clear about who will be involved from their side and yours.
- **Identify the most important gaps** in knowledge, experience or skills – life is too short to be unfocused.
- **Focus on strategy/planning/methodology** – ask key questions and persist until answers start coming, but do not expect everything to happen in a couple of meetings. People need time. Use participatory exercises, such as brainstorming, venn diagrams, mapping and tree diagrams, with large sheets of paper to map out key issues together.
- **Provide training in evaluation and monitoring** so people can discover their own impact, learn and make their own adjustments as they go. Use examples from other projects and encourage visits. Principles of good management apply to all programmes, so don't be limited to just visiting other HIV work.

Build national leadership

Almost all ACET work has been led by nationals in their own nation, and all programmes are accountable to their own national boards. Some ask how we find all these quality leaders. It is relatively easy. Make sure the work is owned by strong, local churches. Church leaders in developing countries rarely feel a complete sense of ownership of a project if the main leader is from a wealthy nation. They usually value the international links, which help with extra funding, but they also know that if supporters back home are unhappy with the way the expatriate is treated, they could cut off that funding.

But why should local churches commit their own best leaders, members of their eldership teams, accountants, lawyers and business people? They may sit back and let the expatriate leader struggle to build his or her own leadership team, often with yet more expatriates from home. If you visit projects which are totally 'owned' by local

Managing change – how to do it

In established projects the greatest challenge can be getting people to change.

The first step is ID (Inspirational Dissatisfaction). If everyone is happy, why would they change? You need to create dissatisfaction by explaining the problem, giving a clear vision of how you believe life could be better.

Consult with others who may be affected, so people begin to own changes together.

Explain what is on your mind, help them understand how you think it will work, listen to their concerns (and then listen loads more), work out together a way round problems, and try to agree together what the next steps should be.

Peter Okaalet, MAP International

churches, seen as part of their own mission, you are much more likely to find strong indigenous leadership wherever you look.

Sometimes local leaders may be ready and able, but do not want to push themselves forward when the expatriate leader is looking around for someone to hand over to. Local leaders may feel great loyalty and affection for the expatriate leader. They may be concerned about hurting the feelings of the expatriate by seeming too keen to see them leave the country. They may feel that they should be humble and have the attitude of being willing to serve, rather than appear to be ambitious to lead the whole programme.

Some leaders who have come from wealthy nations still shake their heads. 'It is not that simple,' they tell me. But as I have seen many times, the painful reality is that they often have to totally leave the situation before local churches sit up and realise that this is *their* work and if *they* don't take hold of it, it will collapse and close. Of course this has happened before on a large scale when governments have thrown out all expatriate 'missionaries'. But even though such changes have happened suddenly and on a very large scale, history shows that local believers usually rise to the challenges and the work continues, although perhaps the model is altered to a more locally sustainable one.

Of course, when leadership changes, many other things change. And we should welcome this: new vision and direction is important to keep organisations fresh. Existing leaders need to trust God for the work as they hand over.

Sometimes I have heard shocking things from expatriate workers such as: 'I don't think there is anyone I really trust in this town/city/ area.' If that is the case it would be better if they went home straight away. What can they contribute if that is their attitude? Who invited them to come? If they did not trust the person who invited them, they should never have agreed to go in the first place. They have just made a very serious accusation against the entire Christian community. Such comments are a sign of tremendous arrogance, ignorance, racism and imperialism all rolled into one.

Now of course there may be unfortunate experiences. Corruption can be a way of life in some places and there may be genuine major leadership shortages. But we also need to recognise that theft from projects is also common in the UK, and major deception/fraud has also happened in philanthropic foundations in America.

Another way to solve leadership shortages can be to encourage nationals who have gone to other nations to return, even if only for a limited period, to help get things started. This is how ACET Uganda started, and is very effective because you have a leader who understands not only the local situation, but also something of the strange cultures of donor nations.

So then, we have clear objectives, the AIDS programme is growing, the team is strong, the volunteers are committed, we have spare capacity to grow – what now? We need to look at developing resources: finding donors and supporters who will help finance the work.

The role of faith-based organisations in delivering government objectives

The experience of PLACA in Nigeria

Due to the high HIV prevalence rate of 8.5 per cent in the Plateau State at the end of 2001, the state government established Plateau AIDS Control Agency (PLACA) in 2002. PLACA exists and seeks to enable people in the Plateau State of Nigeria to:

- have appropriate information on HIV and AIDS;
- have knowledge on HIV and AIDS, as well as to mitigate its impact;
- know their HIV status in order to make informed decisions and to change attitudes from risky sexual and social behaviours;
- participate in educating people who are yet to be reached;
- provide care and support to people with HIV, orphans and vulnerable children and sex workers.

Major successes

Because of PLACA, Plateau was the first state in Nigeria to develop and promote a fully fledged multi-sectoral response to HIV/AIDS in Nigeria and to establish a world class state-owned HIV and AIDS research centre in Nigeria, named 'Plateau State Human Virology Research Centre'. 97.6 per cent of the 3.2 million people of Plateau State have been reached and are aware of HIV and AIDS. 35 per cent of the population of the state have been educated and have knowledge on HIV and AIDS. 31,280 pregnant women have had access to Prevention from Mother to Child Transmission (PMTCT) services. 426 voluntary counselling and testing sites have been set up in the state and are being used for HIV counselling and testing services. Over 22,000 HIV counsellors have been trained and are involved in community-driven HIV counselling and testing services. Nearly a million people have been counselled and tested and know their HIV status. 19,933 with HIV are currently on treatment. 172 support groups have been formed for people living with HIV.

Challenges and lessons learned

Few faith-based organisations are involved in the fight against HIV and AIDS. As a result, the state is being confronted with a high rate of HIV and AIDS related stigmatisation and discrimination. But when the faith-based community is in the driver's seat of the HIV and AIDS response, many people will be reached easier and faster.

Recommendation

HIV is a human virus and AIDS is a human disease. To overcome them, there is a need to use the power of the gospel which God gave to the church community in Luke 4:18. To achieve this, it is recommended that the faith-based community should unite to respond to the AIDS challenge to humanity. God empowered the church community in Matthew 28:18–20 to be in the driver's seat of HIV and AIDS response.

Dr John K. Jinung, Executive Director, PLACA, Nigeria, February 2009

CHAPTER FOURTEEN

RESOURCING THE WORK IN A SUSTAINABLE WAY

So how do we find resources to enable the HIV programme to continue and hopefully to grow? And how do we manage better the limited resources we have?

To living by faith or rely on fund-raising . . . what is God calling us to? Hudson Taylor in China never communicated his own financial needs. Yet in the Old Testament we read that Nehemiah went straight to the king. What is God calling *you* to do? Is there agreement on this within your programme?

If you feel called personally to live by faith or to 'live dangerously' (i.e. make financial commitments that look foolish on paper), you may need to recognise that others may feel called to plan 'responsibly', and to fund-raise, etc. These things must be talked through and agreed on, especially with the church leaders or board to whom you are accountable. And be careful of other people's reputations. For example, if two different HIV programmes linked to your organisation close suddenly because they run out of money, it could destroy donor confidence elsewhere. They may wonder if other programmes are as 'badly and irresponsibly managed'.

A strong faith dimension is vital in every step we take in Christian projects, every decision made, every job we fund, every project we start. There has to be balance between faith and strategy. We need to live as though everything depends on us but pray as though everything depends on God.

Better financial control means that projects survive

Poor financial control is one of the most common reasons why great projects close down and why donors and governments may feel certain projects are not reliable enough to have as partners. It is not enough to pray and hope that God will answer your prayers. Farmers have to plant crops. Builders have to follow safety regulations. Project leaders have to make sure they manage their finances with sufficient reserves, and balance their accounts.

It is vital for projects to do a cash-flow forecast, and update it every month or two. Make a column for each month. List all income you expect, all expenditure you are planning, and calculate the difference between them. Show what the bank balance is at the start of the month and what it should be at the end. You will end up with 12 columns. At the bottom of each month you will see whether you will still have money in the bank.

You may not know all the money you will receive, but you can make an estimate based on what has happened in previous years, and everything else you know. If the estimate is very uncertain, then hold back some of what you are planning to spend until the situation is clearer.

Cash-flow forecasts help focus prayer: you can see exactly what you need to pray you will receive by what dates. Such forecasts are really important. If you are serious about developing a professionally respected programme, it is not enough to just plan one month at a time, using what comes in. For example, you may need to sign a contract on an office, or pay regular salaries or other bills. You cannot do this responsibly without planning ahead.

Managing highs and lows

Even if you know that your income and expenditure will balance out over the year, be careful. You may have major expenditure at the start of the year, and large grants which do not usually arrive in the bank account until the middle or end of the year. Cash-flow forecasts show if you will have enough reserves to manage these kinds of things. Well-funded projects can easily run out of money because of timing issues. It can cause a crisis, because leaders just hope for the best and then suddenly cannot pay bills. Finances must be managed very carefully, or you will damage the reputation of your project – or even destroy it altogether. Donors do not like to be told a project has run out of money because no one planned ahead properly. They are less likely to fund you in future.

Build reserves – for project freedom and security

That is why it is so important to build a reserve, which is money in
the bank at the end of the year that can help you manage finances.
Even things like a change in exchange rates, which alters how much
local currency you get for $100, can plunge a project into crisis
unless there is a reserve. You can easily find that a large grant turns
out unexpectedly to be 10 to 20 per cent less than expected when it
actually arrives into the bank account.

Check exchange rates regularly as you plan budgets – at least once
a quarter. Just keep an eye on these things. Warn donors early that you
think you may not be able to deliver all that you promised if exchange
rates continue to alter in the wrong direction (of course, you can also
have a nice surprise).

Be sure not to confuse reserves with restricted funds. You could find
you have $10,000 unspent at the end of the year, but it was all meant
to go on, say, buying a new vehicle. You cannot use it therefore for
any other purpose such as paying salaries. Even if your project runs
out of cash in its 'general account', if you spend the vehicle money on
salaries, you will probably end up in real trouble, because the donor is
soon going to be looking for photos of that vehicle and wanting to see
it in action.

I have known projects in real crisis with loads of money in the
bank, none of which they can spend on their monthly core costs such
as office, phones, director's salary and so on. That is why reserves can
only be saved out of general funds, which you are free to spend on any
part of the work. It can be very hard to build up reserves, since most
large grants have to be spent to the last dollar within each financial
year. Reserves can come from things like church donations, individual
gifts, subscriptions, income from training programmes, income from
providing consulting services to other organisations, and from trusts
and companies that really believe in the work enough to give you an
unrestricted donation.

In the UK the Charity Commission recommends a general reserve
which is large enough to fund at least three months of normal running
costs. Why? So the organisation does not suddenly have to close down
because of a short gap between one funding commitment and another,
for example. Such a reserve seems an impossibly large amount when
you start, but as you pray, God can do amazing things. Just be

disciplined and don't suddenly expand your programme activities the moment more general income arrives.

Your accounts should show restricted and general funds at all times, and what is needed and when for each separate project area. Put time in now to set up better, regular financial reports, make sure you understand them, and save yourself a nasty shock in future.

Protecting reputation and preventing fraud

Every project in every nation is vulnerable to staff stealing money using tricks and deceptions (fraud). If you don't see any in your own work, you may need to look harder! Such attacks can be really clever, go on over a very long time before detection, and may involve huge sums of money. It is always shocking, upsetting and hurtful when it involves a trusted staff member; even more so if the person has seemed to be a committed follower of Jesus.

Your accounting systems need to be really strong in order to:

- protect your own reputation from accusations;
- reduce opportunities and temptations;
- relieve pressure on staff members, who may have been asked for help to pay for things like life-saving operations for family members (in some cultures there is little understanding that money given by a donor for one purpose CANNOT be used for any other purpose);
- help reassure donors.

You may need help to do a formal risk assessment on a regular basis. What are the weaknesses in the current systems? How can you tighten up procedures? If someone wanted to steal money from the project, how could they do it? Ask for help and advice from larger organisations to learn how to do better.

Help stop fraud – checklist for every project

- Have a detailed audit trail – receipts, everything signed for, detailed records, up-to-date information – and keep a fully computerised accounts system.
- Use independent professional auditors to do a full audit each year. Their audit reports will contain advice about how to improve your systems, which you must follow.

- Expect visits (if you are a larger project) at short notice by an appointed representative of the main donor, not only to look at the work, but to check the accounts.
- Use two signatures for all but the smallest payments – at least one should be a board member, and they should not both be members of the same family or household – to protect staff, volunteer and family reputations from false accusations.
- Bank all income through the organisation's official bank account.
- Do not run other bank accounts unless there are very strong reasons for doing so, approved by the board (it makes accounting more complicated).
- All expenditure must be made through the same account.
- Never use any money from the organisation's bank account for any other purposes or investments (even as a short-term loan) unless expressly authorised by the board. In many nations, making such investments is illegal unless they are zero risk (e.g. putting money into a higher interest deposit account with a national bank).
- Be *very* careful about exchange rates. Do *not* gamble project funds by trying to guess where the markets will go next. You will never succeed for long when betting against professionals who trade billions every day. It is usually safest to keep money in your own national currency – then at least you know what you have. Remember that grants promised in another currency may produce a lot less than expected if exchange rates change, so be cautious in budgeting.
- Give copies of bank statements to board treasurer, book-keeper and director each month.
- The board treasurer should have a close working relationship with the book-keeper so that the book-keeper can quietly raise areas of concern if needed, and the treasurer can help supervise the accounting processes. Be aware that a book-keeper may be under huge pressure not to warn of irregularities, for fear of losing his or her job, or worse.
- Lock away cheque book at all times when not in use.
- Minimise use of cash.
- Ensure all decisions affecting leaders' own benefits or salaries are decided by an independent board, where none of those making the decisions have any direct financial interest – they should not themselves be employed or paid consultants for the organisation, nor any member of their family. This protects your reputation.

Consulting fees and other payments

Consulting fees can be a great way to build up a reserve, as the money the project receives is general income. It should be made clear, when a full-time senior team member is appointed, what happens about consulting fees and other payments that may be made by other organisations for the person's time.

The safest way to handle things is for all contracts to be made between organisations rather than individuals, with payments made payable to the project bank account, and therefore seen by the board in the accounts.

The board may wish to take these factors into account when working out the correct salary for the person each year. If you do not do this, you may find a project leader is spending more and more time working for other organisations and pocketing large sums of money in addition to their official full-time salary.

Things can be complicated if the staff member is part time. It is vital that whatever guidelines are agreed about future working arrangements they are confirmed in writing, with the agreement of the board.

Aim for transparency, simplicity, efficiency in everything

Efficiency – this means that donor agencies all agree if possible (may take some effort to get this) on:

- Common accounting requirements – including agreement to accept same annual date for accounting, even if not coinciding either with the donor's own year end or the anniversary of the grant. It saves so much time and money.
- Common opinions on accounts – there is no point, for example, in Tearfund and Christian Aid sending independent auditors of their own into the same project within weeks of each other. It is a complete waste of effort.
- Common governance/board requirements.

If it all goes wrong:

- *Immediately* involve your independent board. Start by phoning the chairperson today!
- Take immediate action with your chairperson to contain the

situation or deal with the problem, including police involvement if laws have been broken. Some projects are afraid to involve the police, but if you do not, the person is likely to get another job and rob another organisation – and you will be partly responsible. If you take no legal action, it also sends a message to other workers that it is perfectly safe for them to steal from you, as the worst that can happen is they will lose their jobs.

- Rapidly inform your key donors about what has happened and what action is being taken. They will find out anyway, and may have useful advice.
- Investigate how it happened and look urgently at ways to reduce the risk of similar things happening again.

Finally, do keep a sense of proportion, and look at the whole situation before deciding what level of discipline should be taken. I remember a cook who was working in a house belonging to a large, well-funded project. She had given many years of faithful service to the work. One day, she was caught stealing a small bag of rice.

She broke down and wept. It turned out that her sister had died of HIV and she was now trying to feed not only six children of her own, but also five of her sister's, all living together in a small shack. The project had been paying her a very low income – hardly enough for her to survive herself. Her family was hungry. She was desperate. What would you have done in her situation? I am not saying she was justified in stealing. What she did was wrong. But why was she being paid so little? Why did the project not know about her home situation and try to do something to help?

Accountability, monitoring and evaluation

Accountability is a biblical principle, seen in the early church. It is the first thing to look for in any leader. Are they humble and open to correction? Accountable to others regarding the project? Accountable to the leadership of their church in their personal lives? The first lesson in sustainability is accountability.

Weak accountability and governance is one of the commonest reasons for project failure. It is lonely being a team leader, and it is easy to lose perspective. Every leader has character strengths and weaknesses, but they are often not able to see them themselves.

Accountability requirements and structures vary from country to country. To be safe, project directors should be accountable to an independent team of people (a board) outside the immediate situation, who are wise and more experienced. They are there to oversee the director. The stronger the board, the stronger the project will be. Weak boards easily lead to major problems – in finance, team relationships and moral issues.

Board members should ideally *not* be paid by the organisation (it would be illegal anyway in many countries). If board members receive payment from the director, their independence may be compromised or appear to be compromised. Again this is also about reputation and protection from accusation. If some board members *are* paid, it is vital that they are a small minority, and they are not the ones responsible for signing cheques.

And every board also needs a strong chairperson. Such a board/group has different names in different nations: trustees, charity board, non-executive council and so on. Directors sometimes fear loss of control, but they can suggest board members they like, trust, respect and want to work with.

Internationally accepted 'best practice' for boards

The role of the director is to run the organisation and manage the office team and all day-to-day matters. In countries like India, the UK or Nigeria, the director reports to the chairperson of the board, who is responsible with the board to see that funds are properly used; that the work is high quality, and remains true to Christian values and the objectives of the organisation. The relationship between chair and director of the project is very important, for advice, encouragement and supervision. One-to-one meetings are very important, on a regular basis, and a good chair will also know the other senior team members quite well, and spend time with them.

The board has the power to appoint or remove the project director and to approve the annual budget. The board is legally responsible for the correct running of the project, but it should not interfere in day-to-day matters, unless there is a crisis – for example, a dispute among senior staff members.

Some countries have different legal requirements and organisations may be structured differently. For example, ACET Czech Republic is a democratic membership association. Each trained schools worker has a vote, and elects a council to run ACET. The council elects its own chairperson. The director is responsible to the council, and reports directly to the chairperson. But the principles remain the same.

Boards usually need to meet at least once every three months, more often if the situation is changing fast, or in a crisis. Some boards give responsibilities to a sub-group of two to three members who spend extra time on one area, for example finances, between full board meetings. It is really helpful if other senior staff are present for most discussions. It relieves pressure on the director, allows others to make reports, helps answer questions (especially on finances), develops staff leadership, shows you are a team, and helps them understand board concerns.

Different stages of a project, from start-up to maturity and decline/renewal, all need different kinds of accountability structure. There is a need also to adjust to size and budget and speed of change of organisation – with appropriate controls and frequency of meetings.

Summary

Independent boards are vital and if you don't have one you are in danger. They provide:

- Legal responsibility to government for correct running of the organisation.
- Financial/ethical/spiritual discipline/monitoring/guidance.
- A place to ask awkward questions, to challenge and probe.
- Experienced people to guide/mentor/coach main leader(s).
- Insurance against over-hasty and poorly planned decisions.
- A broader and longer term view that makes sense of highs and lows of day-to-day activity.
- A final judge/court of appeal between CEO and senior staff if there are tensions.
- Stability in leadership transitions/succession management.
- Personal support, encouragement, prayer for leader.
- The chairperson, who should also be someone for the main leader to talk to who is close enough to the situation but not part of it (project leadership can be a very lonely experience).

Personal accountability really matters – and is to do with the attitude of the heart, personal lifestyle, family matters. Accountability can be:

- To local church – can be hard if leaders do not share the vision.
- To donors – to deliver on promises made.
- To a community of similar projects or an association – for example, not to act in a way that will damage reputation and work of other programmes.
- To family and special friends – you need their support to be fully effective, so involve them in important decisions such as how often you travel internationally. Allow them to share the big picture, and to care for you. If you are married, do not sacrifice your children or spouse on the altar of your ambition. They are part of your ministry and your witness. How you live is likely to be copied by staff and volunteers.
- To God himself – always!

You may want to meet regularly with a small group of wise friends and a leader from your church on a regular basis, for pastoral support, personal accountability and to pray. If you are married, it may be very helpful to make sure you are there as a couple, so you can be cared for as a household.

How to raise more funding for your work

So you are running a project. You have already found loads of ways to be more efficient, but you think you need more resources. What can you do? The first thing is to pay careful attention to all the things above.

As Jesus said: 'He who can be trusted in small things can be trusted in bigger things' (Luke 16:10–11). Jesus also reminds us that 'to him who has, more will be given' (Mark 4:25). It seems unfair, but the fact is that the stronger a project is, the more funding will come. And the larger you are, the more you are likely to receive (even) more funding – as long as you are careful stewards, able to demonstrate high impact in the community.

But even strong projects can miss great opportunities. Here are important steps to take.

Tell your stories

Many Christians I know are so humble about their work that they are embarrassed to 'boast' about their achievements. They say things like:

'We are only a little church programme, or, 'We have not been working very long,' or, 'We do what we can, but it does not seem very much.'

Jesus said, 'Let your light shine.' Why? So that people may give glory to the Father in heaven. Letting your light shine means telling others how many people you help each year. Tell them if you are (maybe) the only group doing this urgently needed work in your area. Tell them if you are overwhelmed by more requests for help. Tell them if the government loves what you are doing.

Be bold. Be passionate. Let people see. Let them be amazed. Persuade them with good reasons why your project deserves their support. What is so special about what you do? This explanation is your 'Case for support'. Use every tool available, including PowerPoint, with clear pictures, graphs, maps and tables – and only key phrases.

Branding can be an important part of this. Nokia is a brand of mobile phone that people trust. Google and Microsoft are strong brands. Your project name or brand is important and should be a badge of quality that gives people confidence. Wherever they see that name, you want them to relax. They know what you do, your values, your high standards, your Christian foundations, what you stand for. They like your work. If they know of your work in one city, it helps

---

Strong branding – market what you do

ACET Ukraine is only six years old, and has a team of 400 educators working in schools and other situations. They have a strong brand. How did they do it? They do things really well, and make sure people remember their name. They produce a really inspiring 20-minute video every year about their work, as well as beautifully produced brochures and leaflets about drugs, sexual health and caring for those with HIV. They use colourful large flags that they fly at large events in parks or open spaces, or hang on walls at meetings. They print and sell T-shirts, colourful hats, balloons and bags. They publish high quality books. They give every trained educator a signed certificate that looks impressive enough to be framed and hung on a wall. Everything they do tells an attractive story about how they change people's lives.

They appear to others as a great group of people who are making a difference and have fun together. They look really professional and highly organised. It is one reason why they are growing fast. People want to join them and be part of the exciting work. Schools ask for more visits. Government officials know them well. Funders get excited. Church leaders are proud to 'own' them. And their 'brand' has strengthened ACET work in other parts of the region.

open doors in another. If they know of the same name in one nation, it helps gain government support in another.

How strong the Christian element is in your brand will depend on where you work. In some parts of the world, Christian agencies are not allowed to work at all, or find life very hard, and in such places, the brand will look, sound and feel different from in a nation which is mainly Christian – symbols, images, language, tone. Everything we do needs to be adapted to local culture. An influential name can open doors in one country and close them in another.

Target key donors

Christians are often far too relaxed about targeting key donors. They don't bother to do enough research into each one, and their differences. They don't think widely enough about all the different organisations that might be willing to fund different parts of their work. Then they get disappointed at lack of funding.

Donor agencies, companies, governments and individuals all have their own specific interests – usually guided by the personal views of a small number of people. They usually need to give grants of certain amounts by particular dates. They may be under their own pressures to produce results. They may be about to lose tax refunds. Their own budgets for community projects may be cut if they show they are unable to spend fast enough.

Funds bring responsibility. Imagine a relative dies and leaves you some money and you feel led to give a lot of it away. How should you do that? What are the greatest needs? There are so many, it is confusing. Who do you ask for advice?

That is just what it feels like for all donors who have decisions to make. So help them. Serve them in their hour of need. Get close and find out what kind of programmes they are drawn to. What kinds of projects are they limited to? And if your project does not fit their needs, tell someone else whose project just might be a great fit. Read more about this later.

A donor may love your work but only be able to fund one small part of the big picture, and only if properly separated out with its own income and expenditure, aims and objectives, as a clearly defined project within a project. Defining these is one of the most important parts of fund-raising.

How to develop church support for HIV ministry

- Start with your own church and denomination.
- Cultivate friendships with key church leaders to open big doors.
- Take every opportunity to speak at larger forums/conferences and in larger churches.
- Use every volunteer and staff member as a church representative to link to their own church, other local churches, whole denominations.
- Encourage prayer networks – and use SMS/email to communicate urgent requests.
- Explain why regular, small donations are so significant, e.g. $2 a month is $240 over 10 years and $8 a month is almost $1,000 in 10 years!
- Print literature for church use, e.g. World AIDS Day – info packs for preaching, posters.
- Encourage all staff and volunteers to speak regularly in churches.
- Use things like email and SMS as low-cost ways to keep supporters praying/involved.
- Use existing supporters to recruit friends.
- Use church contacts with other nations (tell your story powerfully).

Cluster strong programmes together

Most Christian programmes are invisible to larger donors or government departments because they are far too small. Large institutions like the European Union only give large grants ($500,000 or more). The only way smaller organisations can benefit is by clustering several projects together in joint proposals. When we bury our differences and collaborate it makes a much more powerful story: 'Our partnership of ten agencies reaches 250,000 students a year across three cities with life-saving messages about HIV.'

Large development organisations can often act as matchmakers in a global 'dating agency' between (even) larger donors and projects on the ground. For example, ACET Slovakia recently won significant EU funding, but only as one of four organisations in a group working across four nations. ACET Uganda recently gained funding from PEPFAR (US government), but only packaged up with other projects by Christian Aid. ACET Ireland got funding from Irish Aid when packaged up with other projects by Tearfund. Clustering is a key role of larger agencies.

So co-operate, find out what others are doing, share resources, develop joint plans and present a united front to big institutions. And remember that most of these funding decisions are made in country, by national representatives in local offices. Build friendship and trust with the key people. Invite them to speak at your events. Use them in your training programmes. Invite them to visit your projects. Send them examples of your (excellent and beautifully produced) training resources and suggest a meeting. Be patient. It may take two to four years of quiet relationship building to see results. Find out what kind of projects they are looking for. Don't waste their time with proposals they are very unlikely to approve.

Managing donor–project relationships

Donor–project relationships can cause great joy or frustration. In the best situations we see true partnership. The donor has a problem: they want to help make change happen, and need partners on the ground. Projects have a problem: they are doing amazing work and meeting huge needs in an excellent way, but struggle to meet their monthly costs.

Whose project is it?

Donors often talk about partnership, but what does that really mean? A key issue is ownership and accountability. The donor may feel they have the right to demand all kinds of things. Your project may see them as interfering and time-wasting. Project leaders may feel that requests for detailed reports and accounts represent a lack of trust: 'We are God's workers. Invest in our ministry if you trust us and believe in what we are doing, but when you ask for all kinds of reports, we worry you don't really trust us at all.' Actually such donors are just following international donor requirements, put in place because of scandals in the past and because of UK legislation re fraud and money laundering.

What are acceptable donor demands?

Every project grant should be seen as a 'contract', agreed on the basis of the application made. 'This grant is to fund you to do X and Y in Z area at $ cost, as stated in your plan for the next three years.' It is right that such projects should aim to deliver exactly what they say they will do – preferably a little more. It is also right that projects inform donors as soon as possible if the local situation and needs change. They can then agree together what variations in the plan can be made, before a point is reached when the donors begin to think they have made a bad funding decision, or get a big shock.

These contracts, reports, accounts and so on are also there to protect reputation so that no one can accuse Christian work of being corrupt. They also reduce pressures and temptations. Someone might need to say to a family member: 'Even if I wanted to, I couldn't use project funds for HIV orphans to pay for my uncle's operation – even if it means he will die as a result. The accounts are strictly audited. The donors watch everything, and I would lose my job immediately.'

Imperialism by another name?

Project leaders also need to stand up to unreasonable donor demands – for example, for excessively detailed and frequent reporting. I have seen a single email, written by a thoughtless desk officer, plunge a project CEO over 6,000 miles away into a nightmare of lost sleep for weeks. It is important to inform desk officers of the actual cost in hours of senior project leaders complying with their latest demands. Maybe we should write down the actual number of hours spent on every form or report that is completed. We all need to work together to reduce the time of senior people spent on these things. I am often concerned that long reports may just sit in email boxes or in-trays without actually being properly read.

It is helpful for projects to share experience, and work together to bring some discipline to donors that seem to be behaving badly. I remember when the ACET family met in Uganda in 2005, one global donor sat down in an informal meeting and got a real blast of anger from 12 different project leaders about their terrible processes. Things changed fast.

Government partnerships – how to make them work

In some nations you find the government wants to work in partnership with Christian organisations, and recognises their importance in delivering high-impact, low-cost HIV programmes. In other nations you find the government does not like Christian organisations and is suspicious of churches.

Let us look first at the pressures from friendly governments. Some of them are busy signing large numbers of contracts with Christian agencies, to deliver government services. But are such projects at risk of becoming mere subcontractors to government departments; of losing their calling, values and independence?

There is always a risk that large, successful Christian programmes will become dependent on government grants, and that government will contract more and more services to them to provide. At first sight this seems exciting. But it could be that the only reason for the contract is that church volunteers are working away, giving time for free, so the cost for the service is less than any other agency the government can use.

How to win favour Nehemiah-style

We need to remember that Nehemiah went to see the king to get funding for a religious project – and got it, on favourable terms (Nehemiah 1–2). Here are the lessons from Nehemiah and more recent Christian approaches:

- Be highly professional.
- Show outstanding quality and total reliability.
- Show deep knowledge of government and what they want to do (do your research).
- Show respect.
- Build relationships with key people.
- Get commendations of your work, especially from other government departments or trusted authorities.

It is vital to protect your own culture from too much government control. You will need other sources of income, or the government may rightly feel that they 'own' you. You must have the courage to walk away from negotiations, or government negotiators may sense weakness.

Do remember that even small government grants are very important for credibility/reputation, and will greatly reassure other donors. So make the extra effort. Small grants often open the doors to larger government contracts, but it can take some years for this to happen.

Working in difficult political situations

On the other hand, many HIV projects are working in very tough political situations, where there is effectively no government at all. Political and military instability are common, and go hand in hand with rapidly spreading HIV, and risks in running projects.

It may mean sexual violence, especially against women. Or chaos in transport, banking and communications. ACET teams often work in situations of risk and uncertainty, where other agencies fear to go. For me it is a powerful sign of Christian compassion that they go the extra mile. Those teams have won great respect from local communities and/or government, whether in places like northern Uganda, the DR Congo or Zimbabwe.

Sometimes in extreme crisis situations, project leaders have to work very hard with donors to find new ways to get food or other resources into the area where needed; for example, when banking systems collapse, or there are other administrative nightmares – as happened in Zimbabwe in 2009 where a team was committed to feeding 3,000 orphans with inflation running at 1 billion per cent, and where there was a temporary ban on many development agencies.

Christian organisations may be viewed with suspicion

In some nations all Christian activists are viewed with great suspicion. Remember that words which sound normal and positive in your culture, or within the Christian community, can be badly misunderstood by other people. Be very careful not to create problems for local project workers in such parts of the world. Watch out for insensitive or badly written reports or newsletters; misleading, insensitive or inaccurate websites; ambiguous or confusing SMS messages or emails. It may be that what your website says about the country is correct in the facts reported, but could be very embarrassing to the government. Show respect for national pride, and for laws on respecting leaders. It may be wise not to report some things at all, or only to do so in personal briefings to friends, rather than broadcast by email.

Other governments may be concerned that Christian agencies are being used as a way to spread Christianity in their country, which may be a very sensitive and provocative issue with other religious groups.

Live in such a way that the more people watch or listen, the more amazed they are by your honesty, integrity, good work, kind heart and helpful programmes. They will soon learn of your motivation, your passion and love for their community, your desire to help the government save lives, encourage healthy living and care for those in need.

How to win the trust of governments

- Be transparent and open in what you do.
- Be sure your attitude is always to serve: to help the government in any way you can to solve difficult social problems.
- Seek always to work closely wherever you can with the relevant government departments and co-operate fully with security services when they try to understand what you are doing and why.
- Take every opportunity to be a blessing to those in authority, not a headache.
- Make sure you comply perfectly with every regulation, accounting and tax requirement – not only as an organisation, but also as individuals – especially when it comes to financial records.
- Keep copies of all important documents and records in case of theft or fire or some official taking your computer away for examination – so you can continue to function.
- Develop a good reputation for delivering exactly what you promise, when you say you will do it.
- Make sure every part of your programme is of the highest quality and meets important needs.
- Do not use government grants, referrals, partnerships or collaboration as a means to try to convert people, evangelise, get people to join your church and so on.
- Do not encrypt your emails – it suggests that you have something to hide, when you should have nothing to hide.

Project workers in certain countries should *expect* security forces to take a close interest from time to time, and be *glad* if it happens. Attention may come because they are successful in HIV care or prevention work, they mobilise communities to take HIV seriously, teach a lot of young people about healthy living (so they are seen as influential), are well organised and funded partly at least from outside the country.

Indeed it would be strange if such a project was not being looked at regularly. It could only mean the project was having little impact, or that the officials were not doing their job properly. The closer they look, the more they will find the truth: that here are good people, honest and law-abiding citizens who pay their taxes, keep to the rules and wish to serve their government and nation to help build a better future. Let your light shine, but remember that light will always attract attention.

In nations where it is impossible to register a Christian social agency, a Christian individual can still do HIV work, either as part of the ministry of a registered church (if such activity is allowed) or within secular agencies. Or they may be allowed to register a new HIV agency as a secular organisation, even though most or all of the group of friends who start such a new project may share common Christian compassion, love and commitment to save lives and care for those with HIV.

You may find local officials are willing to be more relaxed about how to apply their rules when they see how good, honest and helpful you are to their community; how you are sensitive and keep a low profile, quietly getting on with your work.

How sustainable is your work?

A lot of nonsense is talked about project sustainability. It's a fashionable concept – to do with environment, community development, personal life. Many donors tell me that they only fund work that is sustainable, but when you probe it is clear that they do not understand the basic principles of development, nor the harsh realities of severe poverty.

Some trusts only fund for a maximum of three years, after which they expect new projects to be fully self-sustaining. Others say 12 months should be enough – even in the poorest nations. But in many places such an approach is naïve, foolish and likely to destroy the very communities the projects are trying to help.

Take Burundi, recovering from ethnic genocide, still unstable, with shellfire heard at night in the capital city. A few years ago three Christian hospitals had the same budget as the entire (broken) National Health Service. The economy is struggling against chaos.

So you give a grant of $6,000 a year to start a new HIV project. You expect the work to grow. And then you are going to cut all funding?

In year 1 the work is only starting. By year 2 loads of people are being reached and the programme is really taking off. Hopefully other donors are gradually giving some support. In year 3 the project has increased its income and taken on more staff, set for further healthy growth, saving lives, caring for people with HIV, mobilising churches, a beacon of light.

And year 4? The project closes. The original donor stops their funding completely, so income halves overnight. Because the donor required every dollar to be spent in the year given, no reserves could be built up. Half the staff lose their jobs and face uncertain futures. Morale is terrible. Schools and clinics feel let down. Reputation is damaged. The team spends so much time managing the crisis that it has no energy left to talk to existing or new donors. The remaining donors start to hear and worry. The work collapses. The director is almost destroyed by the experience and feels he has failed. Crazy. Sustainable?

It could have been very sustainable with a less brutal approach. Suppose funding continued as before for another three to five years. By then the project would probably have grown some more and might be in a position to weather the loss – but only as long as no other donors impose their own three-year limitations.

Some donors add another pressure. For them sustainability means not only achieving total financial independence within three years, but also that every dollar from then on must come only from within the country. This is even more unreasonable than the first requirement and impossible in a country like Burundi.

We also need to think about spiritual sustainability. It is easy to be so consumed in the work that we become too busy to spend time in prayer, in fellowship with other believers, or even in attending church meetings. Yet our work may cause us to reflect more deeply on the teachings of Jesus, giving us a fresh understanding of his calling to the church, and of how we should live.

True sustainability

So what are reasonable aims? First, of course everyone is committed to sustainable development, but let us be clear about what it really means in practice. It is a combination of some or all of the following (the more the better):

- Indigenous leadership – not dependent on people from wealthy nations.

- Accountability to a strong local board – 'owned' by local people as an independent legal entity, not an offshoot of an international agency.
- Raising (most of) own financial support from varied sources.
- Not over-dependent on the wishes of an individual donor.
- Writing own project applications and reports.
- Locating new donors and maintaining donor relations.
- Training new leadership to allow safe growth.
- Strong project management systems in place.

We can add a further two aims – which will happen faster or slower depending on the wealth and economic growth of the country:

- Raising a rapidly growing proportion of total income from sources within the nation – whether government, business, churches, individuals or other indigenous organisations.
- Reproducing within own country or in other nations, having become a centre of excellence that people visit from many nations, to learn from their model and experience.

We must try to stop donor agencies from pretending that they are encouraging sustainability, when all they are doing is passing three-year project commitments to each other, back and forth, as each funding cycle comes to an end.

Another crazy thing is that many trusts only fund new work. So I have seen some projects create work for three years, and the only way they can continue is to close the department down, repackage it slightly and re-launch as a brand new department, funded by the same donor, but run by all the same team, under a slightly different name. I just do not understand how these donors think they can get away with funding so many new things every year without their *own* activities becoming unsustainable. Such policies have 'unsustainability' written all over them.

How to LOSE all your funding without really trying!

- Don't ever get in touch with donors unless you are desperate for money.
- Always make sure you deliver different things than you promised – and late.

- Communicate problems too late for donors to be involved in discussions about adjusting agreed targets and the scope of the work.
- Give inaccurate, vague and incomplete financial information, and only after many requests and deadlines have passed.
- Always make sure you ignore the guidelines donors give you about reporting using their agreed format.
- Complain bitterly when they take more than a week to make a decision.
- Neglect your support base, including local churches and people – don't bother with newsletters, prayer requests or anything else, and turn down church speaking engagements.
- Always wait at least two to three weeks before responding to donor emails.
- Don't bother to meet with other agencies doing similar work in same country.
- Don't check your figures add up in presentations/reports/proposals.
- Ignore risks – don't bother with a book-keeper, don't bother doing the accounts until the end of the year.

Succession planning – leadership for next phase

Remember always that Jesus came as a servant. So you must serve others in the organisation rather than seek to dominate and control everything. Have courage: Moses was a fearless prophet. Plan carefully: Nehemiah was a careful strategist. Character is the secret to long-term anointing/ministry – not great talent (Titus 2:3–5).

A programme is usually only as effective as the whole leadership team, so give close attention to developing your wider leadership. Encourage them with training and responsibility. Spend special time with key leaders each week. Disciple them, just as Jesus did.

We are to serve others in our leadership. We should not be possessive of our role, or hang on to 'our ministry'. All callings are time-limited. One day we will be with the Lord when our physical life is over, and our earthly calling will cease. But many callings end long before physical death.

Sometimes we just need to get out of the way! Maybe someone else has been called to do in future what we are doing now. Seek to empower, train and release others, humbly considering others better

How to raise (more) funds for your project

- People give to people, so build relationships of trust however you can.

- Measure the impact of what you have already achieved.

- Remember that numbers really matter, e.g. pupils reached, people visited at home, how many visits a week, booklets distributed.

- Divide numbers by total costs to get cost per visit, per pupil reached, etc.

- Prove (urgent) need and use emotional stories for impact.

- Show detailed plans to meet need – Structure, Aims and Objectives, Measurable hoped-for outcomes, Costs.

- Show support from respected independent authorities, e.g. government departments, local health officers, other donors, university professors.

- Target right donor for right project – most have many restrictions on what they are allowed to fund. . . which means when there IS a good fit they are likely to be very interested.

- Warm up donors with personal contact/friendship.

- Listen to their *own* needs for strong partners in certain areas of work.

- Think about closest match of their needs with parts of your work.

- Develop specific proposals to help donor with their own problems, e.g. how to increase number of pregnant women with HIV accessing antivirals in French-speaking Africa.

- Create short, clear Executive Summary at front of proposal that tells everything in less than two paragraphs.

- Make sure you know who makes their decisions and their own timetables for process/deadlines.

- Follow up, discuss, adjust to stay true to what God has called you to, and to what they are able to work with.

Peter Fabian, CEO, ACET UK

than yourself. The most important test of leadership is whether we manage to train up others to take the work forward. Remember they will never lead like you do. They are not clones. It will be a new day with fresh approaches.

Different stages in organisations need different styles, characteristics and skills in leaders. Some leaders are brilliant starters who grow new work. Others are brilliant managers of complicated stable organisations. Others are excellent in managing decline, closure, cutting costs.

In the early church there were apostles and deacons. Apostles were responsible for vision, faith and doctrine in the church; for mission strategy and appointing leadership. Deacons served in project leadership roles, making sure that church activities and tasks happened well. This is a useful picture for organisations which are often started by visionaries (social entrepreneurs) but need maintenance by organisers/managers, who are in some ways more deacon-like in function. But it really is important, wherever possible, to retain close involvement with the vision and passion of the founder of your work. The founder's personal story is very significant in most dynamic organisations.

Remember that your successor may be quietly waiting. If the person has a good attitude, they will continue to serve you as leader, not fighting for your job. But that 'servant heart' may mean you fail to realise how ready they are.

When we line up a successor, we need to empower and release them, allowing them to bring different styles and gifting. A gap in leadership is sometimes needed to allow change rather than a smooth transition. The process we use is as important as what finally happens: timing, consultation, fellowship, communication, prayer, commissioning, supporting. We need to be sensitive to the sensations of change – which can vary from relief to grief or both.

Finally: personal survival

HIV ministry often makes leaders vulnerable. A combination of overwhelming need, shortage of resources, pressure for rapid growth, stop-go-stop funding, too much talking about sex (it is dysfunctional and can increase temptations), too much exposure to addiction and brokenness, and being overwhelmed by death, grief, pain, loss of friends, family, neighbours, church members and work colleagues.

And every project worker, volunteer and supporter may have their own opinions about what should happen. It can be lonely, stressful and frustrating.

Leaders often find it hard to get help. They may feel guilt at personal weakness, or be afraid they will lose the respect of workers or be rejected by the church. They may also be afraid they will lose the confidence of donors, or lose their only source of personal income/job.

The 'Sabbath' rest is so important for leaders. It does not have to be on Sunday (often the busiest day of the week for project leaders who are also pastors). Rest can be hard to find. Working from home can blur work and home life, with loss of perspective and vision. There are always urgent emails and issues. But Jesus took time out to pray and rest. We are always more effective when we are refreshed.

If you feel overwhelmed, write down a list of all the things you feel you need to do and pray over it. Ask God to show you which things will have the greatest impact on the situation in the least amount of time and do them first. Sometimes we just need to stop and take time out to reflect, and find God's perspective and peace again. Talk to someone you know and respect – maybe a member of your own board, or a leader in your church.

Some donors have deep pastoral concerns for project leaders, and try to provide support. Some team members in these organisations are very compassionate, experienced, effective and helpful, but we need to recognise that there can be a conflict of interests. However caring the donor representative may be, if they help decide future funding, the project leader may find it hard to share certain things.

A vital key to preventing burnout

You may need to book in your diary twice as many days or evenings off as you think you actually need, to allow for the unexpected. It means you can give away time at short notice and still have personal space and time left for family and special friends. Some leaders do not protect time at all, and then find life becomes overwhelming.

If you are married, your spouse is vitally important and deserves quality time. You are a team together, so take care of each other and invest in your family future, and the whole work will be stronger. HIV work is about relationships, loyalty and faithfulness. It is important that we live out our message, that our marriages are strong, that we are actively involved and rooted in our local church, that our children feel loved and appreciated, that our lives are a prophetic demonstration of our values. So take care of your own relationships. They are a vital part of your own ministry and personal witness.

Your team and volunteers are likely to unconsciously model themselves on your example, so try to make sure it is worth following; for instance, follow your own advice to others about actually taking time off, going home at a reasonable hour.

If you are single, be sure to spend quality time with people you know, love and trust. Invest in those who are part of your own 'family'. You are a powerful prophetic demonstration of how it is possible to be fulfilled as a single person without jumping into sexual relationships or becoming dependent on alcohol or drugs. As a project leader, it can be very difficult, lonely and stressful coming back to an empty home with no one to share the day with. Seek out special people who will be your encouragers on the journey. People who are totally committed to your vision and to you personally. People you can always turn to in a time of personal crisis.

Whatever your personal situation, recognise that frequent trips away from home can weaken you, increase vulnerability, open you to many temptations, and rob you of supportive relationships. Travels also cost time and money. Travel wears you out and may mean you are less easy to live with when you get home. So take care, plan responsibly. Make sure people are praying for you when you travel and are aware of the pressures you and your family/household feel in those situations.

Submit your big diary decisions to family and to others who are wiser and more objective than you are. It is always flattering to be asked to go to another city or country. Try to delay decisions you are unsure about. Other invitations may come in which need to be balanced up. Be strategic, focused and prayerful. Life is too short to waste a single day.

And our prayer in everything should be: 'Your kingdom come, your will be done. May your name be known, may your glory shine.'

TIME FOR ACTION ON AIDS

It is easy to read a book like this one and feel you are not qualified or that there is nothing you can do yourself.

Life is too short to turn up to conferences of church leaders, listen to inspiring speakers and end up simply signing some kind of declaration. Hundreds of pages of nice sounding statements have been signed by tens of thousands of church leaders at hundreds of conferences, summits, forums and consultations about AIDS and HIV over the last decade.

Signing pieces of paper will never change the world. Good intentions, great ideas and hopes will never change the world. Our world will only be changed as men and women start doing things differently; when leaders organise teams, with clear goals and lots of energy.

Life is also too short to waste time reading books like this one unless *something changes* as a result. On the next two pages there is space for you to make your own list of actions that you are promising yourself you will take, by when, and a column for progress. Why not pick up a pen now, and prayerfully write some things there? You can tear the pages out if you need to lend the book to someone else.

Show the list soon to someone you respect, who can hold you accountable to follow through on what you have committed to. Share the list with others you think will be willing to walk the same journey – maybe lend them this book first so they have a chance to respond themselves to what they feel God may be saying to them.

The most important thing of all is to DO SOMETHING

It costs nothing to care, and you need no organising to go and visit a neighbour in need, or to talk to your own relatives about the risks of HIV, or indeed to lend someone this book, or to get involved in an existing programme.

The battle against HIV will not be won by great programmes. It will be won as millions of ordinary men and women in every nation rise up as a people movement, determined to take HIV issues seriously and to make a real difference. And as those who belong to Christ, we have a message of strength and hope, as well as of health and wholeness.

You can't change the whole world, but today you can change someone's world somewhere.

For a list of useful organisations and web links, as well as other resources, please look at the ACET International Alliance website: www.acet-international.org

	Action I will take	By when	Date done	Result
1				
2				
3				
4				
5				
6				
7				
8				
9				
10				

	Action I will take	By when	Date done	Result
11				
12				
13				
14				
15				
16				
17				
18				
19				
20				

ACET INTERNATIONAL ALLIANCE

The ACET International Alliance is a growing community of independent HIV programmes in over 20 nations, which originally began in the UK in 1988. ACET stands for AIDS Care, Education and Training and was founded by Dr Patrick Dixon. Alliance members are united in a common aim to see an effective Christian response to HIV:

- Unconditional, compassionate care for all affected by HIV.
- Life-saving prevention, respecting and upholding the historic teachings of the church.
- Effective training with a holistic approach to personal and community development.

A key part of ACET's work is to mobilise churches and faith-based organisations in effective HIV care and prevention.

The Alliance is a network of organisations seeking to co-operate together on a regional basis, rather than a funding organisation. It does not have a big central administration and does not make central grants.

The Alliance is led by an elected team from India, Russia, Uganda, South Africa, the UK, Ireland and the Democratic Republic of Congo.

Further free copies of this book in many different languages can be obtained by contacting ACET:

www.acet-international.org
email: sheila.dixon@acet-international.org

OPERATION MOBILISATION

Operation Mobilisation is pleased to co-publish and sponsor this edition, and is totally committed to seeing churches everywhere make a compassionate, caring and practical response to all those affected by AIDS and HIV, as well as helping to save lives.

OM was founded by George Verwer. Today, OM is a dynamic, global ministry with almost 3,000 full-time staff working in over 80 countries. It is committed to working in partnership with churches and other Christian organisations for the purpose of world mission. Different ministries of OM provide speakers for churches, conferences and seminars, experienced training in all forms of evangelism, leadership and pastoral care, and a wealth of resources, including videos, books, presentation materials and prayer cards.

www.om.org
www.ombooks.org

UNAIDS

UNAIDS, the Joint United Nations Programme on HIV and AIDS, is an innovative joint venture of the United Nations family, bringing together the efforts and resources of 10 UN system organisations in the HIV response to help the world prevent new HIV infections, care for people living with HIV, and mitigate the impact of the epidemic.

With its headquarters in Geneva, Switzerland, the UNAIDS Secretariat works on the ground in more than 80 countries worldwide. Coherent action on HIV by the UN system is co-ordinated in countries through the UN theme groups, and the joint programmes on HIV.

Co-sponsors include UNHCR, UNICEF, WFP, UNDP, UNFPA, UNODC, ILO, UNESCO, WHO and the World Bank.

UNAIDS helps mount and support an expanded response to AIDS – one that engages the efforts of many sectors and partners from government and civil society.

UNAIDS recognises the importance of faith-based organisations in developing community-based responses to HIV and AIDS/HIV.

www.UNAIDS.org

PARTNERSHIP WITH FAITH-BASED ORGANIZATIONS – UNAIDS STRATEGIC FRAMEWORK

Note by Dr Patrick Dixon, author of *AIDS ACTION*.

I am pleased to include in this book extracts from a very important UNAIDS pub-lication which is a guide for UN agencies, governments and faith-based organisa-tions as they seek to work together. The document shows how vital faith-based organisations are to the strategy of UNAIDS and the opportunities to work in partnership. It was created by Sally Smith, Partnerships Adviser – UNAIDS, working with a team drawn from many organisations.

---

2. Goal, objectives and guiding principles

2.1. Goal

The goal of the UNAIDS–FBO strategic framework is to encourage stronger partnerships between UNAIDS and FBOs in order to achieve universal access to HIV prevention, treatment, care and support, which includes the integration of FBOs in comprehensive national AIDS responses.

2.2. Objectives

The objectives of the UNAIDS–FBO strategic framework are to:

- Encourage global and national religious leaders to take supportive public action in the AIDS response.
- Create strong partnerships between UNAIDS and established FBOs working on HIV.
- Promote strengthened links, including coordination and oversight, with FBOs at the country level to ensure that there is an appropriate interface as part of a comprehensive national AIDS response.
- Strengthen the capacity of FBOs to work on HIV issues and the capacity of UNAIDS staff to work with FBOs.
- Target FBOs not yet working on HIV to include HIV-related activities in their work.
- Mobilize local faith communities to become involved in the local AIDS response.
- Identify and document examples of FBO good practice.

2.3. Guiding principles

Guiding principles for the Global response to AIDS are found in the Resolution adopted by the General Assembly 60/262, the Political Declaration on HIV/AIDS.

In addition UNAIDS partnerships are based upon the following guiding principles:

- People living with HIV must be leaders in the design, programming, implementation, research, monitoring and evaluation of all programmes and policies affecting their lives.
- Human-rights-based approaches, gender equality and the greater involvement of people living with HIV principle are the foundation of UNAIDS' partnership work.
- The value of partnerships must be measured by the extent to which they contribute to reducing the number of people becoming infected with HIV and to reducing the impact on those people living with or affected by HIV.
- The focus of partnerships must be on supporting national ownership, country-led approaches and accountability.
- Resources invested are aligned with and used to support national priorities and to benefit people living with or affected by HIV in the areas of prevention, care and support, treatment and impact mitigation.
- Partnerships must result in institutional and systems strengthening11 (i.e. there must be commitment to strengthen the capacities of national

institutions to provide leadership and coordination in order to achieve universal access targets).
- The best available scientific evidence and technical knowledge should inform the work of partnerships.

5. Roles and responsibilities

5.1. Roles of faith-based organizations

The roles of FBOs in HIV-related partnerships with UNAIDS include:

- Working to end marginalization and HIV-related stigma and discrimination.
- Including people living with HIV in the design, programming, implementation, research, monitoring and evaluation of programmes and in decision-making processes.
- Advocating for universal access to HIV prevention, treatment, care and support services.
- Respecting all human beings as equally worthy of health, dignity and care, regardless of whether they share the same faith, values or lifestyle choices as people of any particular faith.
- Providing services in an open and transparent manner, according to agreed criteria for the handling of finances, serving the community, and monitoring and evaluation.
- Providing services based on evidence-informed practices consistent with the FBO's own faith and values.
- Refraining from attempts to discredit or undermine evidence-informed practices of other actors in the AIDS response.

5.2. Roles of UNAIDS

The roles of UNAIDS in HIV-related partnerships with FBOs include:

- Working to end stigma, prejudice and discrimination in the AIDS response, including a reluctance to partner with FBOs.
- Involving different FBOs in the development of strategy and policy guidelines.
- Involving different FBOs in major decision-making processes and reference groups.
- Advocating for the integration of FBOs in national AIDS responses.
- Advocating, with donors and governments, for planning, implementation and funding decisions to be made in an open and transparent way according to published criteria.
- Advocating for FBOs and other organizations to be appropriately

funded so that they can play a role commensurate with their capacities in supporting the development, implementation, monitoring and evaluation of national AIDS plans.

- Partnering with FBOs in an open and transparent way, respecting their faith as fundamental to their values and activities.
- Monitoring and evaluating civil society programmes in accordance with previously agreed criteria, respecting scientific evidence and the faith and values of FBOs.
- Promoting local community ownership of HIV-related prevention, treatment access, care and support initiatives.
- Leveraging partnerships with other actors in the context of UN reform.
- Refraining from attempting to discredit or undermine religious belief.

5.3. Responsibilities of UNAIDS and faith-based organizations

The responsibilities of UNAIDS and faith-based organizations include:

- Defining the aims and objectives of the partnership.
- Developing and agreeing upon principles (see section 2.3) and a process for working together, which includes:
  - Ongoing communication;
  - The inclusion of partners in decision-making processes;
  - Identifying and implementing activities;
  - Monitoring and evaluating activities, including collecting baseline data, where applicable;
  - Disseminating the outcomes of activities;
  - Establishing a clear exit strategy for terminating the partnership, when appropriate.
- Promoting the value of the partnership to others.

The full text may be found at: http://data.unaids.org/pub/Base Document/2009/jc1786partnershipwithfaithbasedorganizations_en.pdf

FEEDBACK ON THIS BOOK

We are really grateful to the sponsors and organisations that have helped give away over 330,000 copies of previous editions of *AIDS ACTION* (as *AIDS and You*) in over 20 languages. Why do they do it? Because of feedback we get from those who receive the books.

PLEASE HELP US TO HELP YOU AND OTHERS by giving us your comments, suggestions and thoughts. How has this book helped you or other people? Who else would benefit from a copy? Please send your answers to the following questions to the address below, or you can email your replies to: sheila.dixon@acet-international.org

AIDS ACTION – *Feedback Form*

How did you receive a copy of *AIDS Action*?

How helpful is the book for you?

Very helpful   Not very helpful

Quite helpful   No help to me

Have you encouraged other people to read it?   Yes   No

Who?

Has this book changed your attitudes to HIV and AIDS, and to those whose lives are affected?

Yes – a lot   Yes – a little   No

Are you planning new activities or to take new action as a result of reading this book?

    Yes   No

What are they?

Any other comments?

Do you need further copies?   Yes   No

In what language?

How many (if possible)

Who will these copies be given to?

NAME

TITLE

ORGANISATION

ADDRESS

email address (very important if possible)

ACET, P.O. Box 588, Brentford, Middlesex TW7 9BA, UK